THE MAGIC MANIFESTO

ALSO BY BILLY CHAPATA

Chameleon Aura

Flowers on the Moon

Velvet Dragonflies

To All the Women I've Ever Loved

THE MAGIC MANIFESTO

daily reminders
and affirmations
for reclaiming
your magic

BILLY CHAPATA

Andrews McMeel
PUBLISHING®

maintaining your magic is a consistent practice, a process of higher discernment, a deeper realization of your self-worth, a daily act.

many things will blind us from seeing ourselves clearly and threaten to shake our foundations, but how we choose to view and act in those situations informs our inner world and everything around us.

we come across so many different people and experience so many different things that either help us stay in our power or pull us away from our truth, situations and circumstances that help us remember who we are or dull our senses, spaces and connections that amplify our light or decrease its potency.

recognizing and understanding the differences is where the **growth** happens.

absorbing and learning the differences is where the **enlightenment** happens.

accepting and welcoming the differences is where the **magic** happens.

my hope is that each page of this book allows you to reclaim, retain, and recollect pieces of yourself; may each paragraph, sentence, or word serve as a spell over your nervous system that breaks any illusions that made you forget your authentic self.

CONTENTS

equinox.

JANUARY

jump-start my intentions. fuel my
ambitions with energy, and inject
my spirit with warmth. plant seeds
away from my fears and doubts
and closer to my goals and dreams.
bury affirmations on the tip of my
tongue, and hold patience for me
on rough days. keep self-love on
repeat like my favorite song.

JANUARY 1ST

this will be your most beautiful timeline yet.

the life you want to live can begin whenever you want it to, the person you want to be can exist whenever you want them to—the keys to your emancipation have always been in your back pocket. sometimes it takes learning yourself again for you to remember your magic, sometimes it takes shedding who you thought you were for you to see yourself clearly again, sometimes it takes creating a space of acceptance for you to finally see that you can manifest the reality that you desire despite your past, despite your flaws or imperfections, and despite what the world has convinced you you're worthy of. your new era starts whenever you decide it does.

you are the spark, the seed, the catalyst; no one and nothing can ever take that away from you.

JANUARY 2ND

you're a blank canvas with the potential to become whoever you want, whenever you want, in whichever way you want. create yourself freely. draw outside the lines, brush through ideas of perfection, paint over ideas of the past as you build a more vivid picture of the present and *become the masterpiece that you want to see.*

JANUARY 3RD

sometimes one day at a time is fast enough.

taking your life a day at a time is a soft act of surrender; it's a gentle art of giving in to the flow, a tender practice of finding beauty in the current moment. hugging the sunrise without the weight of yesterday's shadows or the anxiety of tomorrow's uncertainties. every day is a new opportunity, offering you the chance to paint with fresh colors, to give your horizons a new flavor, to breathe in the simplicity of now. look for the richness in everything around you, and soak in depths of gratitude. *believe in your process,* knowing that every step—no matter how small or insignificant—is part of a much bigger picture. you honor your pace when you live one day at a time, when you show kindness to yourself throughout and allow the universe to unfold its magic in its own divine time.

JANUARY 4TH

there are people who won't fit into the life that you're trying to build.
people who were for you before but can't meet you
at the depth you now call home,
people who once filled you with comfort but now feel like red flags,
people who felt sweet but now leave a bitter taste in your mouth.
you don't have to feel guilty for moving away
from what you've outgrown.

JANUARY 5TH

give yourself some grace
for doing the best that you could through it all.

give yourself grace in the same way the sun embraces the sky every morning, in the same way the moon serenades the stars every evening. grace isn't just a pardon; it's a promise—a gentle message to your heart that you are deserving of forgiveness, of rest, of pause. it's recognizing that your journey isn't about perfection but about persistence, seeing the beauty in all your flaws, noticing the lessons in every single stumble and finding the growth in moments that feel stagnant. allow yourself plenty of room to be human, to flirt with imperfection, to bask in your authenticity. you are poetry in constant revision, and every line of your life is worthy of being read, worthy of being loved, and *worthy of grace.*

JANUARY 6TH

your growth will scare away many people who can't handle the version of yourself that you are becoming. it will scare people who are used to older ideas of you, but it is not your duty to make people more comfortable, it is not your duty to swim in people-pleasing tendencies.

your only responsibility is simply to be, regardless of how that may look or feel to anyone else.

JANUARY 7TH

appreciate the opportunities to exhale during the transitions, to give your mind a break, and to rest your lungs.

when you learn to hold the slower moments, everything becomes a gentle dance with clocks that reminds you to exhale. the silence between heartbeats, the pauses between breaths, the phases when life reveals its true composition—your slow moments are the universe's way of saying, "stop, look, inhale the beauty around you before you miss it." they contain pieces of peace in which your soul can find air and your heart can finally find time to listen. embrace every single moment: *you will never get the opportunity to exist in them twice.*

JANUARY 8TH

you can stop unrealistically idealizing your life now.
you're not missing out.
you're divinely placed and positioned.

the fear of missing out can become a voice that never disappears. if you never silence it, it can become a shadow that follows you everywhere, casting doubt over everything you do. it's a manifestation of insecurity, the ache of wondering if what you have is enough. it can become a thief of presence, robbing you of the beauty in your now, pushing you to chase illusions, losing yourself in what could *be* instead of embracing what *is*. your path is designed divinely for you, your journey crafted by all the steps you take and not by the ones you don't. the world is packed with endless possibilities, but peace is found in the present, in the love you cultivate in the here and now, in the dreams you curate and create with your own hands. release yourself from the grip of fear, and trust that you are exactly where you need to be. your story is unfolding at its perfect time, in its perfect way; *what is meant for you will never pass you by.*

JANUARY 9TH

your happiness matters.
never make yourself a supporting character in your own story.

placing your feelings on a shelf is reminiscent of being the last page of a book you've written but never read; it's like dimming your sunrise to light someone else's day while you wander around in the darkness. *you can't be the hero you need to be for yourself if you're too busy trying to save everyone else.* when you neglect your own needs, the spark that ignites your magic starts to fade away slowly, starts to lose its effervescence, starts to lose its potency. prioritizing yourself is an act of love that reflects back to you when the world sees you treating yourself the way you deserve to be treated.

JANUARY 10TH

allow them to misunderstand you
while you anchor yourself in your power
and continue to swim in your truth.

being misunderstood can be one of the greatest gifts if you allow yourself to be open to the realization. the frequencies you operate at won't be caught by everyone, and the energy you give off won't be received by everyone, but this is what separates the ones who deserve to experience you from the ones who can't handle you in your entirety. your feelings won't always be validated, your ideas won't always resonate with everyone, your energy may be too cold or too warm for others, but *there is magic in seeing yourself clearly when the rest of the world doesn't.* their lack of understanding for who you are, what you've been through, or what you have to offer isn't an indication of your worth—your true power lies in how deeply you understand yourself.

JANUARY 11TH

always remember that your peace is not worth sacrificing for people who have no idea of the fires you've had to walk through to find it.

your journey is sacred, distinctive, unique. it's a bittersweet narrative of resilience, a beautiful testimony of your strength, an ode to your growth. those who truly understand what you've been through will honor the wars you've fought and the mountains you've had to climb without having to minimize your experiences. they will see the depth of your past mirrored in your old chapters, feel the hints of your struggles in your spirit, and hold space for your healing with love and softness. release yourself from those who are dismissive of your pain, the ones who trivialize your scars, the ones who demand your peace without understanding the battles you've waged to protect it. your peace is precious, a hard-earned treasure that deserves to be cherished by those who truly see you for all the gold that you possess in your soul.

JANUARY 12TH

you'll know it's not for you anymore
when it pulls you away from your authenticity
more than it pushes you toward it.

the world will try to mold and change you into something more palatable, but find comfort in knowing that what is meant for you will fill you by honoring your tastes, resonating with your soul, allowing you to breathe freely and stand firmly in your authenticity. there will be no need for masks or pretenses, only room for honesty, softness, and the kind of love that doesn't require performance. what is in true alignment with your spirit will not demand that you reduce or diminish your magic in any kind of way. it will not ask that you dilute or dissolve your essence away; it will only amplify your voice, making it a clear testament to the beauty of unapologetically being yourself. trust in what flows, and *allow your authentic self to be the compass* that guides you to what is truly yours and leads you away from what isn't.

JANUARY 13TH

sometimes forgiveness will be more for you
than it will be for them.

more softness with yourself, more kindness to your older self, and more acceptance for what has already happened. *dwelling on the past won't do anything but poison your roots,* slow you down from growing, fill your spirit with resentment, and eat away at your peace. dwelling on the past won't change the winds, but holding a space of forgiveness for yourself will. you are worthy of forgiveness regardless of how wounded or regrettable your past may look, and despite the mistakes or bad choices you've made, you are deserving of the gift that comes with being able to let go of it all to welcome in a healthier future for yourself.

JANUARY 14TH

real wealth is found by seeking value from within.

richness was never outside of you; it has always been within. the journey is inward, a search for the treasure chest buried deep in your soul. prosperity has nothing to do with what you own. it is measured by how deeply your spirit reaches, how brightly your light continues to shine, and how tenderly you care for the peace blooming within you. gold can be found in your authenticity, jewels are unearthed in your truth, pearls can be seen in the wisdom you carry. this is the wealth that cannot be stolen, the wealth that moves with you through every season. let it steady you through every rise and fall, a reminder that what you are searching for has always been inside—waiting for your eyes, waiting for your arms, waiting for your light.

JANUARY 15TH

the wind may not be blowing in your direction currently,
but maybe this is not an indication that you're stuck.
maybe this is just a sign that it's okay for you to change
the route you were originally heading in,
even if it takes you a little longer to get to your destination.

there's always magic happening behind the scenes, even in your most uneventful moments; there's always growth taking place in the shadows, even in your slowest of phases; there are always lessons to be absorbed, even in your most painful stages. *trust that everything is unfolding for you, just in time.* in sequence with your intentions, in line with the work you've put into yourself, in tandem with what you deserve. it may feel confusing when the waves are not flowing your way. it may cause impatience when things aren't manifesting in the way you intend, but it will all make sense eventually when the universe finishes painting the picture that you're meant to see.

JANUARY 16TH

love should never cost you your peace.

love should be a sanctuary, a gentle haven where your soul finds rest. in its purest form, it should be a soothing balm, not a source of turmoil; it should wrap you in a warm blanket, ascend you to new heights, and decorate your heart space with tranquility. when love flows with your spirit, it becomes a refuge that never requests the sacrifice of your peace. anything that disturbs your stillness is not love but an illusion wearing its name. true love uplifts, it nourishes. it stands by your side, never against you. *love should be a garden where your soul blooms,* not a storm that uproots it. allow yourself to be found by love that complements your inner harmony, and gravitate to the love that feels like a homecoming.

JANUARY 17TH

you'll lose many things when you start being honest with yourself.

the losses that come whenever you're being true to yourself are the sacrifices that pave the way to the freedom you deserve. whenever you choose to look into mirrors filled with honesty, every illusion and mask falls away, revealing the unfiltered composition of who you are and what is for you. honesty with yourself demands courage because it means letting go of the comfort built on familiar lies and detaching yourself from expired narratives. you will lose connections that were built on a shaky foundation, lose sight of paths that were never yours to tread on, and lose identities that delicately disguised your genuine self, but these losses are simply rites of passage, clearing the space for the authentic you to finally make an appearance. every loss comes with newfound clarity, a discovery of the strength in standing in your truth, a sense of liberation that comes with no longer hiding from yourself. *every loss opens the room for authenticity, inviting deeper connections and more meaningful pursuits.* welcome every loss as a necessary step on the road to who you need to be, knowing that what remains after all the shedding you've done is pure, magical, and real.

JANUARY 18TH

it's never too late to start swimming in water
that helps you float instead of drowning you.

too many times you've left your self-worth unattended while trying to fulfill everyone else's needs; too many times you've neglected your happiness while trying to make everyone else comfortable; too many times you've freely given out energy that you should've given yourself, but it's time to come back home. it's time to recommit to where it all starts, it's time to recommit to the real priorities, it's time to recommit to where the love really begins, *it's time to recommit to you.*

JANUARY 19TH

be patient with the masterpiece you're becoming.

it's not about having it all figured out at once. even the most beautiful structures were built piece by piece, brick by brick, with patience and persistence. exercise gentleness with yourself as you navigate through the cosmos, knowing that mastery is a journey, not a destination. applaud your progress, however small or minuscule, and honor the unique set of tools you now carry. with patience and love, you will find that *you have always had what it takes to create the life you've envisioned.*

JANUARY 20TH

stop downplaying your intuition.
you're feeling what you feel
at this precise moment for a divine reason.
trust it.

unsubscribe from your doubt. trust your intuition more, trust your feelings more, trust your experiences more, trust your gut more, trust your body more, trust yourself more. exercise discernment, but never feel guilt for doing so. many times we're shown signs about something and feel vibrations deep down that validate those sentiments but ignore the feelings out of fear, lack of love for self, or self-doubt, but this is your sign to start paying more attention to what you've been putting off. don't pay the price tomorrow for things you ignored today.

JANUARY 21ST

sometimes what you see as an inexplicable disappearance is really just a divine intervention.

some losses are not really losses. sometimes the things that we think are meant to stay are the things that harm us the most. it's not until they are purged from our life that we truly see how much we've gained from their removal. everything you lose is not without reason, everything that disappears is not by coincidence, everything that doesn't stay isn't to be held on to. *take what is no longer by your side as a good omen;* it is only creating space for who and what you truly deserve.

JANUARY 22ND

enjoy the smaller moments on your journey.
this is how you remain present
when it all feels mundane.

the transitions in your slowest phases can be the hardest pills to swallow, but trust that there are always things happening for you, even in stillness, even in moments when you feel like you aren't going anywhere, even in moments when you feel like you aren't achieving anything, even in moments when you feel stuck. perhaps this phase has something to teach you, and once it has come to pass, you will feel like you again; perhaps once you've absorbed the waves, you will feel movement again; perhaps once you've understood the lessons in this momentary pause, you will feel growth again. *trust your transitions.*

JANUARY 23RD

you are worthy enough as you are.
you are deserving enough as you are.
you don't have to alter pieces of who you are
just to be loved or accepted.

it's a perilous path you take when you change yourself to be accepted by other people. it's an uneasy expedition, a journey that leads you away from the core of who you are. with each compromise, each alteration, and each adjustment, you give away a piece of your soul and silently erode your true essence. anytime you make the decision to change yourself to fit other people's expectations, you sacrifice some of your magic, you become a shadow of your true self, you water down the vitality of your individuality. acceptance gained at the cost of your identity is an expensive price to pay; it keeps you stuck in cycles where the fear of rejection dictates your every move. but hold on tightly to your authenticity. the ones who are in alignment with your light will see you for who you are, not for who the world expects you to be. *let go of the desire to change for anyone else's validation* so you can find the freedom and peace that comes with being unapologetically you.

JANUARY 24TH

managing who has access to you is how you maintain your magic.

not everyone deserves parts of you. not everyone can handle parts of you, and not everyone will be able to accept parts of you, but your discernment is what keeps your flame burning and lights the way toward who does. finding balance requires you to be honest with yourself about which connections take away from your power and which ones amplify it. your *accessibility is a privilege,* and you have every right to be cautious about who is allowed to consume doses of your magic.

JANUARY 25TH

slow growth is still growth.

however long it's taking for you to reach your destination or achieve your goals is not an indication of your worth or what you deserve. slowly detach yourself from the habit of self-sabotaging all the hard work you've put into yourself by watering all the seeds you've planted with impatience. everything that's taking time is merely preparing you so that when it finally finds you, your arms can handle the weight of everything you've been waiting for.

JANUARY 26TH

you are not responsible for how people perceive you.

break free. people's perceptions of you aren't your reality to live in. if you don't tread carefully, what people think of you can become crippling to your self-worth, it can wear down the fabric of your spirit, it can become the reason you remain stagnant in your growth. the more you release yourself from the boxes that people try to fit you into, the closer you get to unwrapping your true essence and finding your authentic self. resist becoming a prisoner to people's ideas of who you are; *how anyone falsely perceives you isn't your burden to carry.*

JANUARY 27TH

even your worst moments have something to teach you.

even your lowest situations in life are packed full of lessons and epiphanies, dressed in hidden blessings and wrapped in adversity. in the depths of all your lows are seeds of resilience waiting to be found, keys to knowledge waiting to be discovered, sparks of growth waiting to be lit that will illuminate your path forward. your darkest moments will require you to dig inward; they will require you to be honest with yourself until you unearth the light that has been hiding in the corners of your soul. life's roughest moments are the crucible in which you are forged and the alchemy that transforms your pain into power, your chaos into clarity, and your wounds into wisdom. trust that *even in the worst of times, there is something valuable to be gained,* a hidden gift waiting just for you.

JANUARY 28TH

planting and watering the seed doesn't always mean that your garden will grow the way you want it to. cultivating your plants consistently by giving them attention and sunlight doesn't always mean that your crop will sprout the way you want it to. *sometimes all you can do is focus on what you can control* and let go of what you can't while trusting that everything that isn't going to plan will have a fundamental lesson to teach you.

JANUARY 29TH

the story you consistently tell yourself will always be more important than the narrative they try to write for you; the ideas you hold of yourself will always be more important than the distorted ideas they impose on you. anyone who hasn't experienced your chapters fully will only be able to judge you by your cover and ignore the substance within the pages that make you, magically, you.

JANUARY 30TH

your wholeness is yours to fill.
your cup is yours to replenish.

hold claim to your own narrative. sew the tapestry of your existence with threads of accountability and self-love. no one else can fill the spaces within you that crave understanding and acceptance. your wholeness comes from embracing every part of your being: the light, the shadows, the wounds, the scars. it's the commitment to heal, to grow, to honor your journey without waiting for someone else to complete you. it's when you self-reflect, gently devote to self-care, and set firm boundaries that you begin to take responsibility for your happiness. *you are the architect of your own completeness.* the power to feel whole lies in your hands and not in the temporary validation anyone can offer you.

JANUARY 31ST

accomplishments and failures are not tied to your self-worth.

the things that go your way and the things that go left are merely chapters in the story of your life, not the essence of your entire being. you are more than the sum of your successes and mistakes, more than your risings and stumbles, more than your victories and setbacks. you are the dreams you hold, the love you give, the perseverance you carry in the marrow of your bones. never let the highs or lows of life define you; they are just waves in the vast ocean of your existence. stay grounded knowing that *you are enough just as you are* regardless of what happens or doesn't happen for you.

FEBRUARY

engulf me in clarity. open my
heart to things i refuse to see, and
shine light on things that need to
be accepted. soften my fear of the
unknown and give me resistance
anytime i am tempted to put my
hands on the wheel of anything
i cannot control. wash away my
doubts, and magnify my truth.

FEBRUARY 1ST

you are an experience.
who you let into your life
and who you keep out
should be reflections
of how you want your inner world to look.

you are a living, breathing wonder of depth that not everyone deserves to be a part of. your journey is a library of dreams, passions, and truths that unfold to tell a captivating story. anyone who's been lucky enough to witness your experiences should also be able to appreciate and respect the things you've been through. your existence is invaluable, a deep adventure, rich with lessons and insights, full of beauty and splendor, shaped by love and vulnerability. your presence is a gift, a blend of emotions and experiences that deserves to constantly be celebrated. place yourself in the company of those who are aware of your value, the ones who uplift your spirit, the ones who appreciate the unique path that you're on. your time and energy are precious, and you have every right to protect your space from those who do not recognize your worth. it is not your duty to accommodate everyone, nor is it to fit into spaces that can't see you for who you truly are. detach yourself from those who aren't in alignment with your growth, and continue to shine knowing that *your selectivity is not selfish; it is a means of survival.*

FEBRUARY 2ND

the biggest shifts come when you realize that things aren't always going to go in the direction you want them to, but that holding a space of kindness for yourself and what didn't come to fruition is how you *grow through the cracks.*

FEBRUARY 3RD

when you try to force alignment, you end up attracting comfortable distractions instead of what's actually meant for you. you end up drawing in experiences that taste good in the moment but don't fulfill you in the long term. allow what's for you to *flow* into your life.

FEBRUARY 4TH

make peace with the reality that some connections are only seasonal regardless of how you try to dress them up. accept that some people are only temporary regardless of how permanent their impression feels. release energy that wants to leave if your growth is pushing you in two different directions.

FEBRUARY 5TH

reserve your attention wisely.

your energy is a valuable resource, a vibrant current that fuels your soul and lights up your path. it's vital to protect it, guard it, nurture it. it's important to invest in relationships that find different ways of nourishing it. surround yourself with those who pour into you as much as you pour into them because they can't stand the sight of seeing your cup empty if theirs is full. these are the people who see you clearly, the people who celebrate your highs and hold you during your lows; these are the ones who understand the value of your energy, the ones who respect your boundaries and appreciate the work you've put into yourself. in reserving your energy for those who recharge you, you honor yourself and your magic; you cultivate a life filled with meaningful connections, oozing with the love and support that you truly deserve. feel no guilt for letting your energy flow to where it is held with soft hands.

FEBRUARY 6TH

loyalty isn't more important than accountability.

it's in the balance of both loyalty and accountability where the foundation of true connection is formed. genuine energy is always rooted in transparency; even if the truth stings, even if it tastes sour, it carries the sentiment to hold each other accountable for the sake of becoming better versions of each other. *accountability is the mirror in which we see our true reflections,* the compass that helps us navigate through our imperfections while we learn from them. it's a deeper form of love that stresses honesty, even when it's difficult, even when it's uncomfortable, even if something changes. without accountability, loyalty loses its integrity, becoming a facade that can crumble under the weight of silence or unspoken truths. so if you ever have to lie to yourself to preserve a connection or to keep the peace, know that it *isn't* and was *never* for you to begin with.

FEBRUARY 7TH

re-create yourself shamelessly,
as many times as you need,
as many times as you desire,
as many times as you see necessary.

you're a multidimensional and multifaceted being, and *you're allowed to re-create yourself as many times as you need.* there comes a time on your journey when it may be necessary to embody a different version of yourself, a version more in tune with the sounds your spirit makes, a version more in line with the direction you're headed in, a version more fitting of the person you're trying to become, but attach no guilt or shame to your need for transformation; your growth is not at anyone's disposal but your own.

FEBRUARY 8TH

you will never have to abandon who you are
if you're rooted in the right places.
you will never have to sabotage your growth
if you're occupying the right spaces.
you will never have to step outside of who you are
if the connection is right for you.

FEBRUARY 9TH

there is much more to you than your mistakes and missteps
you are not solely everything that has gone wrong
for you or where you've fallen short
you are not a mixture of anything that
collapsed or times you've felt defeat
there is so much *goodness on the way* for you to drink in

FEBRUARY 10TH

sometimes the real strength is found when you *stay in your frequency* instead of lowering your vibration to match theirs. sometimes the real power is in choosing to remain true to who you are even when their energy tries to take you out of your element.

FEBRUARY 11TH

you haven't been able to shake that feeling
because that feeling is meant to be there.

we get the call so many times, in our moments of fear or doubt, in our moments of clarity, in our moments of confusion, in our moments of realization, but choosing to ignore the call is only a betrayal of self. sometimes what we feel might be an overreaction, paranoia, overthinking, a delusion, anxiety, or a trauma response when it is actually a call to look at our feelings a little more deeply. why do they exist? why are you feeling them? what's triggering you? why is a specific person or place evoking these emotions? why are you receiving this message in this exact moment? our past and experiences will always play a part in how we process certain things in real time, but your intuition is more powerful than you think, more present than you're aware of, more necessary than you give it credit for. give yourself the time to explore what space your feelings are coming from. when you get the call for deeper discernment, never ignore it. *stop sending your intuition to voicemail.*

FEBRUARY 12TH

even when you think you're missing out, you never really are.

be patient with this masterpiece you're becoming. you'll go through many lows before you see the progress you're trying to make, experience much confusion before your path starts to make sense, feel isolated before you're surrounded by truth again, but it's all part of a bigger plan. sometimes we get so wrapped up in the need for instant gratification or the desire for immediate success that we miss out on the valuable lessons that come in our waiting period. your season is just around the corner, your blessings are on the way, *all in divine time.*

FEBRUARY 13TH

your step back is not detrimental to your journey. *see it as an opportunity to take a breath,* take it as a chance to recollect yourself, take it as a moment to absorb the lesson before being able to carry on your voyage with a better understanding of who you are and what your unique situation requires from you.

FEBRUARY 14TH

it's always been you.
you've always been love.

celebrating you, celebrating partners, and celebrating any intentions to attract any potential connections in the future. today can be beautiful for some people and difficult for others, but whether you're spending today in your own company or with someone special by your side, know that you are worthy of celebration simply for being you, know that your wholeness is not defined by anyone's presence or absence, know that *you are love* whether someone is pouring into you or whether you're pouring into yourself. may your well never run dry whether it's being refilled by someone else or whether you're cultivating that love for yourself.

FEBRUARY 15TH

you can never truly embrace the weight of tomorrow
if all you're doing is holding on to
the heaviness of yesterday.

what's done is done, what's ended has finished, what's run its course has concluded, what can't be changed isn't meant to be. sometimes we delay our healing or progress by holding on to energy that is meant to be released. not everything will be easy to let go, and not all memories are easy to erase, but coming to terms with what's happened regardless of what we could've done differently is how we tend to deep wounds and break challenging cycles. find the courage to stop drowning yourself in what can't be changed so you can start floating in energy that supports your growth and your future.

FEBRUARY 16TH

be kind to yourself.

sometimes we navigate through the world with a compass pointed outward, seeking validation and approval in the reflection of others, but what if the most crucial direction we need to face is inward? what if the most important direction we need to turn to is toward ourselves? it can feel like a foreign concept when the kindness we so readily extend to friends and strangers is directed at ourselves, but self-compassion is the fertile ground from which all other forms of love can truly blossom. showing yourself softness isn't about blind indulgence or ignoring mistakes; it's about acknowledging them with patience and grace and offering yourself the same understanding you'd give the people you care about and the people you love. understand that *true kindness starts within;* it's the inner melody that guides you through life's various soundtracks, a constant reminder that you are worthy, capable, and deserving of love especially from yourself and regardless of all the less desirable things that you've been through.

FEBRUARY 17TH

having the right energy means nothing if you're giving it to the wrong spaces, the wrong things, or the wrong people.

you can be radiating brightly, a fountain of enthusiasm and support, but pouring yourself into people who drain your spirit is only a recipe for frustration. they are energy vampires sucking the joy from your efforts, opportunists hoping to absorb air from your presence, or perhaps people simply incompatible with your magic, but their energy is counterintuitive, a wet blanket smothering your flame. it's not about being cold or withholding your natural essence, it's not about being passive and diminishing your authenticity; it's about learning to choose better, learning to exercise your wisdom. *it's about discernment.* think of flowers, their faces perpetually turned toward the sun. they don't waste their energy chasing shadows; they seek the source of life-giving light. in the very same way, you deserve to be surrounded by those who bask in your glow, appreciate your warmth, and reciprocate it with their own good vibrations.

FEBRUARY 18TH

you will never have to filter your energy for anyone who appreciates the full picture of who you are.

there are people who meet your awkward silences with understanding smiles, who find the hidden rhythm in your offbeat humor, people who don't flinch at your vulnerabilities but see them as threads of strength, people who aren't intimidated by your truths and who view your raw honesty as the bow that binds the two of you closer; this is your community. they are not mirrors reflecting a perfected version of you but open windows letting in the full spectrum of your personality. with them, conversations become a delightful dance, not a minefield to navigate. you can be your most enthusiastic self, your most contemplative self, all within the same breath. they celebrate your victories with an intensity that matches your own and, during your stumbles, offer a helping hand without any judgment. *the people meant for you will never demand a performance* from you; they will demand only that you come as your full and authentic self. the ones who offer you this space deserve to always be held close.

FEBRUARY 19TH

i can never be stripped of my truth if i consistently clothe myself in love.

even when surrounded by those who may not understand or oppose your truth, *dressing yourself in self-love empowers you to remain in your magic,* it allows you to express yourself genuinely with compassion and not defiance. those who try to dispossess you of your truth are powerless against the radiant force of love; it exposes their own fears and insecurities, making their attempts to control your narrative useless. dressing yourself in self-love doesn't guarantee that everyone will accept you, but it grants you the freedom to live authentically, to let your truth shine through with confidence. it allows you to build connections with those who cherish your honesty, creating a haven where your truth is celebrated and not ostracized. your truth is the essence of who you are; it is the life-stream of your intentions, the lifeblood of your uniqueness. clothe yourself in love and it becomes an invincible shield, protecting your spirit while allowing your true self to radiate outward to the rest of the world.

FEBRUARY 20TH

at times, you will doubt yourself when you
are doing what's best for you
you will be uncertain of yourself when you
are taking care of your self-esteem
people who can't comprehend your actions
will look at you from a blurry lens
but it's always worth noting that *keeping certain people at a distance*
doesn't make you a bad person if your intentions are good

FEBRUARY 21ST

they'll be either curious or intimidated by what they can't understand.

you carry a constellation of experiences, beliefs, and quirks within you, a personal dialect that shapes how you navigate the world. sometimes you'll encounter people who simply don't speak your language. that dissonance can be intimidating, trigger feelings of detachment, and cause you to lose sight of yourself. people often shy away from what is difficult to decipher and what doesn't fit neatly into their existing frameworks, so there's always a chance that your brilliance, your complexities, and your uniqueness might be perceived incorrectly. but *being misunderstood isn't a flaw; it's an invitation.* it's an opportunity to patiently translate your unique dialect for those willing to learn; it's an opportunity to let the people who speak a similar language find you and build common ground with your soul's dictionary. don't douse your flame for anyone's comfort. embrace the mystery you embody. the world needs more people like you. it needs the beautiful unsolved puzzles that only a select few are able to figure out.

FEBRUARY 22ND

disconnect what still connects you to the past you're trying to heal from.

sometimes we cling to the energy of past relationships, the warmth of a bond that has since cooled. we romanticize memories, yearning for what existed before, even if it means sacrificing our own well-being in the process. but *revisiting expired energy is like trying to mend a cracked vase with dried flowers;* it might seem beautiful for a moment, but the foundation still remains broken. the bitter truth is that some connections simply reach their natural conclusion. people grow in different directions, priorities shift, and the energy that once flowed freely now stagnates. holding on is like clutching a deflated balloon; it offers no life, only a reminder of what once was. healing requires you to let go; it requires acknowledging the past with gratitude for the lessons learned, then gently placing the box full of memories back on your mind's shelf. invest in the present, in the relationships that nourish your spirit and challenge you to grow. only then can you truly heal your wounds and embrace the potential magic that awaits.

FEBRUARY 23RD

your small wins are still signs that you're headed in the right direction on your journey.

some wins may not be grand pronouncements—they might be the quiet satisfaction of simply getting yourself out of bed, the unexpected compliment about your appearance, or the conquered fear that held you back from a particular conversation—but never dismiss them as insignificant. they are not irrelevant feats but divine guideposts on your journey. each small win is a testament to your resilience, a confirmation that you're moving in the right direction. it's a much-needed message from the universe reminding you, "you've come this far, and you have the strength to keep going." these victories, however small, should fuel your ambitions, they are the sparks that ignite a fire meant to burn away self-doubt and propel you forward; they remind you that progress, even if baby steps, is still progress. the vastness of the journey can be scary, but don't lose sight of the beauty in the small moments. celebrate the climbed mountains, the chaotic waters you swam through, the moments you eclipsed your perceived limitations and surpassed your own expectations; this is the proof and validation that you are, indeed, on the right path. so gather your small wins, let them be the stars in your darkest phases, guiding you through the lows, reminding you that your destination, though distant, is closer than it seems. keep moving forward, for each step, each victory, no matter how small, brings you closer to your dreams and where you want to be.

FEBRUARY 24TH

the greatest betrayal comes when you abandon yourself to go the extra mile for someone who wouldn't even walk halfway for you. return back home and rest your feet for a while; *save your energy for people worth the trip.*

FEBRUARY 25TH

your low moments have a way of dimming the light around you
they have a way of sapping the brightness emanating from within you
forgive yourself for how you moved during the phases when you
weren't seeing yourself clearly

FEBRUARY 26TH

cut the cord energetically when it adds more noise than peace to your spirit, plug yourself into spaces that recharge you instead of depleting your essence, surround yourself with people who recognize your light and brighten it when you're running on low. *manage your magic.*

FEBRUARY 27TH

you've never been behind in your journey.
you've never been lacking in your progress.
you've always been right on time, even when you felt in misalignment.

at times, it feels like the world is one giant game of comparison. we watch as others glide through milestones and accomplishments and allow their achievements to poke holes of uncertainty in our hearts. the thought of falling behind and missing the cosmic train can cause many fears, but what if clocks on the wall aren't the only timekeepers? what if there's an angelic melody sounding and a divine soundtrack that guides us each at our own tempo? *your timing is carefully constructed,* a unique blend of preparation and opportunity. trust that the universe has a plan, a rhythm for your life that unfolds in perfect timing. you are right where you are supposed to be, gathering the experiences and the wisdom to create your own symphonic masterpiece.

FEBRUARY 28TH

leaving behind what doesn't serve you anymore is an art.

some things are meant to be felt, absorbed, and understood but never to be kept. if it eats away at your peace consistently, holding on to it won't ease your chaos, holding on to it won't calm the waves, holding on to it won't ever fill your plate with relief; all it will continue to do is steal your smile and block any potential pathways of growth. learn to let the universe take care of what you can't control so the energy doesn't build toxic and unstable foundations within you; learn to find pockets of gratitude for knowing the truth so you can move forward lighter, with no illusions under your belt.

MARCH

cover me with robes of clarity
and wrap my intentions in velvet.
give me the awareness to see what
shouldn't stay and the courage to
open the door for what needs to
leave. allow me to find my breath
again in places that don't suffocate
my truth or authenticity.
be abundant.

MARCH 1ST

i am finding my groove slowly,
even when the music switches tempo and the melodies feel unfamiliar.

sometimes for miles, sometimes for moments, we drift further away from ourselves. life has a strange way of blurring the edges of our identity, leaving us lost in a deep ocean of expectations and perceptions, but within the waves and the changing current, a truth always prevails—the potential to rediscover yourself. by peeling back old layers, shedding skin you've outgrown, revisiting the passions you may have forgotten about, and remembering melodies that once resonated with your soul, you inch closer to your truth. rediscovery isn't about erasing the past but about integrating it. you are not the same person who once traveled with a backpack full of masks and disguises but an evolved version, wiser and full of awareness. the world may seem to have moved on in your absence, but maybe it was awaiting the return of the authentic you, with your newfound clarity and self-awareness. bask in the exquisite magic of becoming reacquainted with the extraordinary person you always were.

MARCH 2ND

remember that you haven't come this far by accident.

all the detours, all the reroutes, and all the setbacks weren't mistakes; they were twists and turns you needed to bring you to this very moment. each wrong turn you've taken was a lesson, and every obstacle you've encountered was a teacher, so *never diminish your journey by attributing it to mere chance or coincidence.* you've made choices, sometimes with vivid vision, sometimes in the blinding fog of uncertainty, but each choice, each decision, each step has only brought you closer to seeing the clearer picture, even when your moves felt unintentional.

MARCH 3RD

you can't do anything with their envy, hate, or misunderstandings.

consistently assuming responsibility for what other people think of you will always leave you feeling exhausted, drained, or misunderstood. some people will only be able to see you through scopes that they recognize or viewpoints that feel familiar, but *it is not your duty to compartmentalize yourself into something other people can accept or understand.* focus on the perception you have of you, and let them form whatever narratives they please. whatever book they've written for you isn't yours to read.

MARCH 4TH

anytime you have to convince them of your worth,
you lose a bit of potency in your magic.

flowers have never pleaded for anyone to notice their petals; the sun has never begged for anyone to feel its warmth; trees have never asked for anyone to observe their growth, so why should you live any differently? your being was never meant to be explained or justified. you simply exist, just like the stars in the night that continue to shine regardless of whether anyone looks up or not, *just like the ocean that doesn't need to persuade anyone of its depth.* your worth has never been up for debate, and you have never needed anyone to validate your magic.

MARCH 5TH

there are many things you could've handled differently, but those things are done now, those events are etched in history. work on forgiving yourself and holding a space of gentleness until you feel softness oozing from your regrets and your mistakes.

MARCH 6TH

where you are may not be where you want to be,
but where you are
is where you're supposed to be.

the thunderstorms you face will pass, just like the sunshine after them will fade; the tears you cry today will dry, just like how the laughter that fills your heart will melt into silence. embrace the universe's impermanence. this is what makes each moment precious, this is what gives your life more depth, this is what adds color to your horizons. hold on to nothing too tightly, for everything is transient, everything is always shifting. grief will soften, anger will dissipate, and happiness will find new ways to fill you. everything temporary is a gentle reminder that we are all on borrowed time, so cherish the present, savor its beauty. *trust in the shifts;* you will get to where you want to be eventually.

MARCH 7TH

don't let this chapter you're stuck in
convince you that the rest of the book isn't worth reading.

life will throw you curveballs, unexpected events that will leave you with bruises—a connection crumbles, a dream feels like it's slipping through your fingers, a mistake casts a long shadow of regret. it's natural to dwell on these chapters, to fear that their darkness will stain the pages in your story forever, but *a bad chapter doesn't erase the beauty of the ones that came before it.* don't become its prisoner, and don't let its energy hold you hostage by reliving the hurt and despair on a loop. acknowledge your wounds, learn from all the pain, and turn the page to reveal the potential on hold. you are the author, the pen is firmly in your hands, and you have the power to shape your story in whichever way you desire.

MARCH 8TH

celebrate the divine feminine.
applaud the creators of life.

celebrating the unseen, the underappreciated, the misunderstood,
celebrating the superheroes, the divine feminine, the healers.
celebrating the nurturers, the warriors, the mothers, the daughters,
celebrating the sisters, the partners, the friends.
celebrating women, *today and every day.*

MARCH 9TH

you will not find happiness by peeking at the plants growing in someone else's garden.

happiness isn't found by watching someone else's peaks with envy. it blossoms from appreciating the unique sight before you, the lush jungles you've traveled, the breathtaking sunrises you've witnessed, the resilience it took for you to reach this point. comparison always breeds discontent because it overshadows your own accomplishments, it minimizes your hard-earned victories, it puts blockers on the magic flowing in your veins, it fuels a relentless pursuit of something that may not even exist, an illusion of happiness built on someone else's foundation. start shifting your gaze inward; appreciate the strength that brought you here. you have your own beautiful journey to focus on.

MARCH 10TH

constantly swimming in old memories
won't make the waves return.

love in its purest state is a constant current. it's a force that pulls you in, not a stagnant pool you revisit. it thrives on growth, but when that ceases, it starts to weaken gradually; laughter becomes strained, comfortable silences grow heavy, the connection that once sparked feels like a fading flame. some connections ebb and flow, and when their journey reaches a natural conclusion, that doesn't diminish the beauty of what once existed. honor the memories, the love that was there before, and then, with a gentle breath, *release it all to make space for the new beginning you deserve.*

MARCH 11TH

you have survived every tornado, wildfire, and thunderstorm that has threatened your peace, but here you are still standing. *do you not see that there is a bigger reason why you're still here?* allow time to reveal what kind of magic the universe has in store for you.

MARCH 12TH

what's for you won't require you to rush who you're becoming to attract it.

the things that are intended for you won't demand urgency; they will simply acknowledge the importance in your unfolding, honoring the pace of your journey by respecting the sacredness of your process. embrace the slow drip of your becoming. trust that *what's for you will meet you where you are,* in your own season, in your own time. let go of the rush, the haste, the pressure. what's truly yours is already aligning with your essence. it awaits you with open arms, just as you are, patiently anticipating your arrival.

MARCH 13TH

there is life after your mistakes.

every time you release the heaviness of the past and latch on to the light in the present, the freedom to move forward with an unburdened conscience can finally be found. it's in the acceptance of your past—with all its imperfections and lessons—that you begin to unshackle yourself and set yourself free. forgive yourself for the roads you didn't take, for the words you left unspoken, for the mistakes you made when you operated at a lower level of consciousness. each of these moments was a necessary part of your journey toward becoming who you are today.

MARCH 14TH

i am deserving of a life that flows in tandem
with my ideas and my intentions.

you are deserving of a life that does not battle with you but flows. a life that pays attention to the rhythm of your ideas and honors the sincerity of your endeavors. you are not here to drag yourself upstream, to exhaust your soul in battles with currents that were never yours to follow. your peace is not in resistance, but in alignment; your joy is not in control, but in trust, and when you choose to live in tandem with the truths you carry inside, you will discover that the ocean was never against you—it has only been waiting for you to loosen your grip and let the waves take you home.

MARCH 15TH

knowing yourself will scare anyone that has yet to find out who they are.

when you spend time truly getting to know yourself, you become a beacon of authenticity illuminating every path in front of you with your magic. this can be intimidating to those still wandering in the mist of their own insecurities, the ones still figuring out who they are, the ones who haven't met themselves yet. *the knowledge you carry of yourself is a mirror* reflecting both your light and your shadows; it reveals the depths of your being, the courage it takes to face yourself, the bravery it takes to accept every facet of who you are. this can unsettle anyone who has yet to embark on their own journey inward, those who are still grappling with their own reflections, but your light should never be seen as a threat; it should be an invitation for others to begin their own exploration and find the vulnerability to discover who they truly are. your self-awareness will be misunderstood by those who still don't know themselves, but you are not obligated to dilute yourself to be more consumable to anyone.

MARCH 16TH

where you've been planted is not where you must always remain.

beginnings are not prisons; they are simply the soil where you first took root. your growth is too important to be buried in stagnancy. you were not meant to shrink yourself just to fit familiar ground. you were not meant to keep pouring life into places that no longer nourish you. staying the same might feel safe, but safety can become a slow burial if it costs you evolution. the version of you that you're becoming needs room to stretch, room to bloom, room to reach toward light you've never known. sometimes that means moving on from old spaces, old roles, and old versions of yourself that no longer fit. it's okay to outgrow what once felt right. it's okay to leave the soil that raised you when it no longer sustains you. it's okay to seek more light, more space, more possibility. honor where you've been, but do not confuse it with where you're meant to stay. your roots were meant to grow, to travel, to explore new ground. your becoming deserves movement.

MARCH 17TH

let the dust settle so you can see what the storm was trying to teach you.

when the weather in your life feels out of control, it's hard to see clearly; emotions swirl, thoughts clash, and everything feels like chaos, but bad conditions don't last forever. in the aftermath, when the winds die down and the instability fades, lessons remain, waiting to be discovered. take a breath, a moment, a pause. in the stillness, clarity emerges. the storm was not just a force of destruction; it was a teacher, disguised in turbulence; it came to shake you, to wake you, to show you what was hidden beneath the surface. look closely at all the debris. what is still standing? what was swept away? there, in the remnants, are the truths you need to see. storms reveal what is resonant within you, what you truly value, and what you need to let go of. lessons aren't always obvious at first. sometimes you need to sit with silence and discomfort to truly understand the messaging around you.

MARCH 18TH

may your choices be rooted in happiness so sweet fruit can grow from your intentions.

choosing happiness is an essential act of self-love, a declaration that your serenity matters. when you fill your own cup, you have more to give to the people around you, more to give to the world, more stored for yourself when you need it in reserve. making choices that prioritize happiness is about living in alignment; it's about waking up with a sense of purpose and going to sleep with a sense of peace. it's about the little things that make your spirit sing and the moments that make your heart dance. your happiness is not meant to be compromised for the sake of anyone else's expectations because *joy is your birthright.* every choice won't be easy, every day will have its own unique set of challenges, but prioritizing your well-being, your dreams, and your essence will help you carve out a life that feels more like yours, one in which the warmth of happiness feels close by, even if the sun feels distant.

MARCH 19TH

find the magic in spending time with you.

solitude isn't isolation; it's a deliberate pause, a rare chance to shed the masks we wear for the world, a chance to drop the disguises we wear to make other people comfortable. creativity begins to flourish in those silent corners, dreams start to take shape, whispers of your soul slowly become audible. solitude isn't a rejection of connection but simply a preparation for it—a unique chance to recharge your batteries, recalibrate your senses, and cultivate a sense of inner peace that you can then share with the world. you return to your relationships, not with codependency, but with a newfound clarity and a heart brimming with the quiet joy of self-discovery. allow solitude to be your sanctuary, a space where you can simply be; *the deepest connections often begin with a deep understanding of yourself.*

MARCH 20TH

release the guilt that comes with prioritizing yourself.

letting go of the guilt associated with self-care is like untying the knots in your shoelaces. it may be a little time-consuming and cumbersome, but it allows you to proceed on your journey without tripping over yourself. it's a radical act of kindness, not just toward yourself but toward the ones you love. a garden that is depleted of self-care cannot give sustenance to others, and *a heart overflowing with guilt cannot offer anyone a genuine connection.* guilt might convince you that you're neglecting your responsibilities, that others deserve more of your attention, but an abandoned well eventually runs dry, too. by refilling your own cup, you ensure that you have something to offer others. prioritizing yourself is an act of responsibility, a way of ensuring you can show up for yourself and for those you love fully.

MARCH 21ST

resentment is poison, but gratitude is medicine.

resentment is a thief, stealing joy from the present and tainting memories of the past. it's a toxic concoction that warps your perception of the world once you ingest it. it wraps around your heart like tight vines in the spring, slowly suffocating your capacity for happiness. it festers within, poisoning your self-esteem and clouding your judgment. gratitude, on the other hand, is an elixir that gives you life; it's a conscious choice to focus on the blessings that are currently in your possession and the ones that are yet to come. choosing to take a spoonful of gratitude isn't about ignoring challenges or minimizing hurt. it's about acknowledging the difficulties while focusing on the lessons learned and the strength gained. it's about appreciating the good in your life, even in the presence of hardship. gratitude nourishes your spirit; it allows you to forgive past transgressions, both real and perceived; it allows you to see your worth without lack; it fills your heart with a sense of peace and empowers you to move forward with a renewed sense of optimism. let go of the bitterness that weighs you down, and hold on securely to the appreciation for what you already have.

MARCH 22ND

you are not required to be kind and subdued all the time.

your heart is vast and complex, an ocean of emotions that ebb and flow. it's okay to feel anger, to feel hurt, to have boundaries. kindness is a gift, not an obligation, and you are allowed to protect your peace. sometimes the kindest thing you can do is be honest with yourself. acknowledge your limits, your needs, your truths. you don't owe your kindness to everyone, especially at the cost of your own sanity. *kindness is beautiful, but so is self-respect.* you are allowed to take up space, to express your feelings, and to stand firm in your boundaries. kindness comes from a place of abundance, not depletion. forced kindness born from obligation is not kindness at all; it's a mask, a burden, a disservice to your own soul. you are not required to be kind all the time, but you are always required to be true to yourself.

MARCH 23RD

your softness is radical.

in a world that can be so unforgiving and unkind, it's magical to remain soft. it's easy to build walls, to harden your heart, to become indifferent, but you choose to remain open, to feel deeply, to love fiercely; *this is your superpower.* staying soft requires you to embrace vulnerability, to allow yourself to be seen, to be touched by the double-edged sword of life. it takes courage to stay soft when life tries to toughen you, it takes resilience to remain tender when your heart has been bruised. your softness is not weakness; it's the bravest thing about you.

MARCH 24TH

loss helps you realize what's there and what's not.
be grateful for the clarity.

in every loss, you discover what you've been holding on to. you learn the value of presence and the fragility of moments because *loss peels back layers,* revealing your true self. it shows you the strength you never knew you had and the resilience buried within your heart; it forces you to confront your emotions, to sit with your grief, to understand the depths of your love and the impact of your connections. in the aftermath of any loss, you see life with a new lens; you appreciate the simple things, the quiet moments, the temporary smiles; you learn to let go of what doesn't serve you and hold on tightly to what does. loss redefines your priorities, giving you a sharper sense of what's important and what isn't. it gives you more clarity, not by diminishing your love or your memories but by enhancing your appreciation for the present, your vision for the future, and the understanding in your own strength.

MARCH 25TH

*what good deeds someone did for you in the past
are never an excuse for their mistreatment of you now.*

your worth isn't a balance sheet weighed down by debts of gratitude that justify disrespect. kindness should never be a currency used to purchase your silence or your pain. your value is inherent, not contingent on the benevolence of others. you are deserving of respect and love simply because you are. past favors don't give anyone the right to dim your light or to mistreat you. *gratitude and self-respect can coexist; you can be thankful without accepting harm.* never let nostalgia blind you to the reality of how someone treats you now. your heart deserves to feel safe, to feel honored, to feel cherished, not to feel bruised by the heavy weight of past obligations. you can appreciate the good they did for you while refusing to accept the bad, because genuine kindness doesn't come with strings attached, and true love never asks you to suffer.

MARCH 26TH

when you become your own muse,
you allow yourself to be
the art and the artist simultaneously.

when you find everything you need within yourself, your happiness ceases being dependent on things that have nothing to do with you, everything around you that adds value to your existence becomes a bonus instead of the oxygen you need to be the fullest version of you. the appreciation you cultivate for yourself echoes through the other parts of your life; it sets the standard for what you deserve and the boundaries for what you don't; it allows the people in your life to see that your bare minimum is reflected in how highly you view yourself; *it allows any potential connections to see that you won't settle for being treated any less than how you treat yourself.* being your own muse allows you to find a deeper self-awareness for your own magic, a deeper understanding of your own power, a deeper love for yourself that doesn't hinge on what anyone else does or says, an unconditional type of appreciation for your own being. lean into who you are already and the unique work of art that you are becoming.

MARCH 27TH

honesty with yourself waters the seeds in your soul.

honesty with yourself is nourishment. it is the rain your spirit has been waiting for. every time you choose truth over any falsehood or pretense, you pour life into the seeds buried within you. keep choosing it, keep feeding it, *keep watering it until the roots grow strong enough to break through any lie you once built your comfort on.* someday, truth won't just be something you practice—it will be who you are.

MARCH 28TH

*it's never too late to leave where you've sat before,
to feed your own needs now.*

your heart is so giving and so full of love, poured out into everyone else's cup except for your own. you've been the rock, the shoulder, the constant source of warmth for others, but in being so, you've forgotten to tend to your own garden, your own desires, your own dreams; it's time to come home to yourself, to remember that your smile matters just as much as anyone else's. *you are not just a backdrop to other people's lives; you are the star of your own.* you deserve the same care, the same love, the same attention you so freely give to others. self-abandonment is not a badge of honor, it's a silent cry for self-love, a request to recognize your own worth. you've been so busy being everything for everyone that you've lost touch with your own essence. it's time to reclaim your space, your time, and your heart.

MARCH 29TH

how you answer this will always tell you if a
connection is healthy for you or not:

is their presence allowing me to maintain my
magic, or is it taking away from it?

is their energy draining mine, or is it allowing
me to remember who i am?

MARCH 30TH

no one truly knows the things you've gone through except for you.

this journey doesn't come with a map that has clear directions; it's an unpredictable path, filled with unforeseen obstacles and hidden detours. every scar you carry tells a story, a testament to the battles you've fought and the resilience you've had to possess. to judge you based on your current position would be like criticizing a sculptor based on a single chip of marble; it ignores the artistry in your struggle, the vision that has brought you this far. anyone who doesn't understand but still chooses to judge is speaking only from a place of comfort, from a vantage point that overlooks the rough roads you've had to travel on to get here. *you are the writer of your story,* the one who has walked the path, felt the sting of defeat, and tasted the sweetness of victory. hold your head high as you continue your climb. let the opinionated voices fade into the distance. you are the author, the hero, and the ultimate judge of your own remarkable journey.

MARCH 31ST

understand that you cannot help anyone find the path back to themselves if they are unwilling to take the first steps.

you can offer people the tools, you can offer them the resources, you can offer them love, but the journey of transformation will ultimately belong to them. you can honor their journey only by respecting their pace and understanding that *you cannot force them to grow or change.* they must be willing to meet you halfway, ready to embrace the possibilities that lie ahead. you can be a light in their moments of darkness and a viable source of support, but you cannot make decisions on their behalf or live their life for them. your only duty is to hold space for their journey without sacrificing your own well-being. allow them to make their own mistakes, to learn their own lessons, and when they finally choose to take the first step, your love and support will be there to help them forward.

APRIL

hold a space of patience for me.
give me the courage to bloom
no matter where i am planted
and the awareness to keep intuition
close when my surroundings
get blurry. illuminate every
space within me that i dimmed
out of fear, impatience,
or lack of self-love.

APRIL 1ST

there is nothing foolish about your ideas.
better to be a fool for trying than full of what-ifs.

there is nothing silly about what resides in your heart or what occupies the space in your mind. the only weight is the story you tell yourself about how others will receive it. the truth is, *silence will never protect you from judgment*—it will only chain you to regret. better to stumble while trying, better to look naive for believing in your own light than to spend your days haunted by the questions you never allowed yourself to answer.

APRIL 2ND

the need to convince them to see your worth
is usually a sign that you still don't recognize your own.

you lose so much of yourself when you beg others to notice you. every time you stretch your hands out for validation, you hand over pieces of your power; every time you attempt to prove your worth to people who refuse to see it, you make their blindness the measure of your light. the moment you stop campaigning for recognition, you start reclaiming your freedom; the moment you stop auditioning for love, you start remembering that you were already chosen, already enough, already whole.

APRIL 3RD

feel no guilt about your need for rest.

rest is not a luxury but a necessity. a vital part of your journey, a necessary component for peace. find no shame in taking a step back, taking a moment to catch your breath, finding solace in stillness. rest is where the healing begins, where your spirit rejuvenates, where your dreams start to take root. find no shame in taking pauses, allowing yourself the space to recharge, giving your lungs and mind time to reset. your worth is not dictated by how much you do but only by the love and care you show yourself. silence the lies telling you that you must always be busy. rise renewed, knowing you are worthy of every moment that allows you to gently inhale and exhale.

APRIL 4TH

you can never overexplain yourself out of anyone's perception of you;
people will think whatever they want to think of
you regardless of what you do or don't do.
live anyway—uninhibited, free, knowing that
whatever they choose to believe has
nothing to do with you but says much more about them.

APRIL 5TH

too often you've waited for other people's approval
to finally recognize your own worth
too often you've waited for their consent to fill your wholeness
too often you've let their acceptance—
or lack of—determine your steps
but you've always been the *catalyst*, even without them

APRIL 6TH

i am flourishing with or without anyone's validation.

growth doesn't wait for applause. it doesn't pause until someone says, "now you are worthy." it doesn't bend itself to fit the timelines people think you should be following. growth moves in its own rhythm and so do you. the danger comes when you confuse silence for failure, or when you measure your journey of becoming against the approval of others. understand this: validation is fleeting. it rises and falls with moods, with seasons, with perceptions. if you tie your worth to it, you will always be chasing, never arriving. but when you decide that your blossoming belongs to you, everything changes. you begin to honor the small wins, the quiet shifts, the subtle breakthroughs that nobody else sees. you begin to recognize that just because no one claps doesn't mean you aren't thriving. trees do not cease their growth because the forest is silent. flowers do not delay their blooming because no one is watching. your journey is aligned with a rhythm higher than public opinion; it is aligned with divine timing. and when you lean into that truth, you'll realize *you've been flourishing all along.*

APRIL 7TH

pay attention to how people react to your happiness or sadness.

in the light of your highs and the shadows of your lows, true colors are revealed; watch who celebrates your victories with delight and who goes ghost in your darkest hours. your happiness is a beacon. those with pure intentions will bask in your glow, uplift you, and dance with you in your moments of triumph. they won't shrink in your flame or try to pour water over it. in many ways, your sadness is a test; true friends, true connections, will hold space for your pain, offering comfort without judgment. they won't turn away when the skies darken; they'll be an anchor, a shelter, a safe harbor. *be wary of those who appear only when the sun is shining.* if your happiness stirs envy or indifference, their intentions may not align with your well-being; if your sadness is met with impatience or absence, it's a sign that their support is conditional and their presence is superficial. how people react to your feelings is a compass, guiding you toward those who are meant to be in your life and steering you away from those who aren't. let it inform your choices, your trust, and your relationships. surround yourself with those who embrace the full spectrum of you, the ones who understand that both joy and sorrow are integral to your journey.

APRIL 8TH

imagine being enough for yourself? what a concept.

imagine waking up and realizing that you are not missing anything. that nothing outside of you needs to arrive for you to feel complete. that you are not an unfinished story, waiting on someone else's pen to write the final chapter. imagine what it would feel like to stand in front of the mirror and not ask for permission to exist beautifully. to not bargain with your reflection, to not tally up flaws, to not weigh your worth against anyone else's. being enough for yourself is cathartic. it is the understanding that you no longer must hand out the keys to your peace, it is the understanding that you no longer need to beg for scraps of love from tables that were never built for you, it is the understanding that *you are the home you've been searching for.*

APRIL 9TH

your dreams stop being dreams when you put a timer on them.

your dreams are timeless, boundless and free; they are not meant to be confined by the ticking hands of a clock or the structured pages in a calendar. putting your dreams on a timer only creates pressure, anxiety, and self-doubt; it makes you feel like you're running a race against the world when you're actually in your own beautiful lane. your dreams deserve patience, love, and dedication. they are like seeds planted in the soil of your soul, needing time to grow, to flourish, to sprout. rushing them won't make them blossom faster but will only rob you of the joy of your journey. life has its own rhythm, its own pace. trust that your dreams will manifest at the right moment, when you are ready to embrace them fully; there is no deadline for your aspirations and no expiration date on your passions. some of the most beautiful things in life take time—*a flower doesn't bloom in a day, a tree doesn't grow overnight,* and your dreams are the same. nurture them with care, water them with persistence, and let them soak in the light of your belief. never measure your dreams against the timelines of others. what matters is your dedication, your resilience, and the faith you carry.

APRIL 10TH

you're not walking away from that low vibrational connection.
you're simply walking back toward yourself.

after being lost for so long and losing elements of your self-worth while navigating through jungles of judgment and oceans of opinions, here you are: stronger, wiser, and thriving. stings to your self-esteem and bites aimed at your being could never poison your progress. *travel back to yourself as often as you need,* at whatever pace suits your spirit, at whatever intensity your endeavors require, so you can see yourself clearly with every return you make back to you.

APRIL 11TH

sometimes choosing to love someone in silence is the best medicine for your soul.

love shouldn't require silence, but sometimes life forces you out of your element. you indulge in connections that splinter like broken glass, leaving you with a heart in need of healing. to protect yourself, you might be left with no choice but to silently love the ones who hurt you. loving them from a distance allows you to acknowledge the past with tenderness, to appreciate the good while acknowledging the hurt, and to move forward with more awareness in your heart. as you heal, you might choose to rebuild the connection on new terms, with reinforced boundaries and newfound understandings, but remember that *protecting yourself isn't selfish.* it becomes a necessary step in your self-care when the ones you love refuse to acknowledge the pain and misery they've caused you.

APRIL 12TH

the more you chase people, the more you run away from yourself.

chasing anyone is a long race that leaves you breathless, empty, and longing; you deserve more than to exhaust yourself for someone who doesn't see the divinity in your soul. those who are meant to be in your life will gravitate to you naturally, drawn by your energy and the glow you emit. you don't need to prove your worth to anyone; your existence is proof enough. never deplete your spirit trying to convince someone of your value. instead, invest in yourself. *when you focus on becoming the best version of yourself, the right people will find you.* they'll recognize your worth without you having to chase them, they'll recognize your light without you having to shine it in their face, they'll recognize your importance without you having to force your significance in their presence. those who truly belong in your life won't need to be pursued; they will stay, they will appreciate, and they will adore you for exactly who you are.

APRIL 13TH

you will never be the same person after you heal.

healing is not necessarily a return. it is not about stitching yourself back into the person you were before the wound. it is about becoming someone new—someone softer in some places, stronger in others, wiser everywhere. and with that transformation comes a shift in vision. you begin to see people differently. you begin to notice what uplifts you and what drains you. you notice who honors your boundaries and who is comfortable only when you abandon them. healing changes your appetite. the things you once tolerated lose their flavor. the spaces you once forced yourself into no longer fit. it can be disorienting at first, realizing that some relationships were built on the version of you who didn't know their own worth. but that disorientation is proof of growth. accept the changes. *do not mourn the parts of your life that cannot follow you into your wholeness.* the shedding is necessary. every boundary you place, every standard you raise, is an act of reclaiming your energy. not everyone will celebrate this new you, but the ones who are meant to stay will rise to meet you where you are. you are not meant to heal into the past. you are meant to heal forward, into the future, into the self you were always destined to be.

APRIL 14TH

you limit your magic when you're led by ego,
you expand everything when you're led by love.

you fall into the darkest cycles when you honor your ego more than the love you have for yourself. the most movement you'll ever experience is when you exercise a space of vulnerability and start being more honest with yourself about the ways you're contributing to your own suffering instead of rejecting the downloads you're receiving. following the path of least resistance is easy when you're being led by your ego because it doesn't require you to look too deeply at yourself and the reasons that brought you to the road you now traverse. ego only adds more weight to your journey if it isn't managed correctly. *lower its intensity, and increase the volume on truth;* you deserve to travel lighter.

APRIL 15TH

when time reveals people's true colors, don't rewind the clock by trying to create a picture of them that feels more comfortable. *you are being shown exactly what you need to see* so you can proceed without any illusions of who they truly are.

APRIL 16TH

love with no agenda attached, and expect nothing in return.

love that thrives on connection and blossoms freely without the weight of demands or desires, love that prospers in selflessness and never feels like a transaction—let love like this guide you. to love without attachment is to mirror the sun in its generosity, offering your warmth and affection openly, without the forecasting of reciprocity. this isn't to imply you should be naive or invite mistreatment; rather it's to recognize that *true connection is born where love is given freely* and received with gratitude. it's about celebrating the other's presence without the need to control or manipulate; it's about allowing the other person to be who they truly are without the burden of expectation; it's about cultivating energy where you are able to float in the love you have for yourself regardless of whether the waves you're giving out return to you or not.

APRIL 17TH

some days will require you to sit with your pain to heal from it
they will require you to ask your wounds questions to heal from it
they will require you to face your demons directly to heal from it
they will require you to stop avoiding discomfort to *heal from it*

APRIL 18TH

i am whole even when they choose to see only half of me.

you have never been lacking despite your circumstances, you have never been lacking despite anyone's inconsistent reciprocation, you have never been lacking despite anyone's misguided narrative of you, you have never been lacking despite anyone's inability to see you fully. everything starts with how you pour into yourself; everything starts with how you treat yourself; everything starts from within, and that determines how everything shapes your outer world. may your wholeness never be defined by anyone's ideas of you or their lack of validation, but instead by how you perceive yourself and how you water the beautiful parts of you that others may choose to ignore.

APRIL 19TH

people won't always share the same passion as you,
and some people will never see the good in your
intentions no matter how hard you try.
don't expect people who only know how
to carry cold buckets of water
to appreciate the fire in your belly.

APRIL 20TH

this metamorphosis is preparing your wings for flight.

transformation rarely feels gentle. it stretches you in ways you didn't ask for, breaks you open in places you thought were sealed, and asks you to release versions of yourself that once felt permanent. sometimes it feels like loss, sometimes it feels like chaos, and sometimes it feels like you are unraveling with no clear picture of who you are becoming. but this is the sacred work. the breaking is not meant to destroy you; it is meant to shape you. the discomfort is not punishment; it is preparation. every rough phase, every difficult stretch, is strengthening you for a life you cannot yet see. metamorphosis is not supposed to feel familiar. it is supposed to feel like departure, like shedding, like stepping into a body you've never fully known before. and even though it aches, even though it demands patience, trust that the process is building something within you that will carry you further than you've ever imagined.

APRIL 21ST

there will be a season when you find your light again
a season when you find your voice again
a season when you find your power again
a season when you find your magic again
a season when you find *you*

APRIL 22ND

discern who is allowed keys to your heart, but always remember never to lock yourself out.

you'll encounter many people who believe they deserve the keys to your heart, but you are not required to hand them over to just anyone. be patient, take the time to know who truly values you, who shows up consistently, who loves you for you. it's okay to hold on to your keys until you find someone who aligns with your spirit, someone who synergizes your intentions, someone who views your heart's safety as paramount. it's not about being guarded but about exercising wisdom from older experiences, it's about recognizing that your love is too valuable to be given away carelessly, it's about avoiding being wasteful with energy that has taken so long to cultivate. *those who deserve the keys to your heart will earn them through action,* sincerity, and support. your love is not for everyone, and you have every right to be cautious about who you let into the walls of your life.

APRIL 23RD

your happiness is not for anyone but you to cultivate.

the longest-lasting connections go beyond the romantic or the platonic, they go beyond time and proximity; *they're rooted in the intention to become the fullest version of yourselves as individuals while putting that energy back into the connection* so you can grow together. there's something beautiful about putting your growth, and your respect for their growth, at the forefront of your union so you can both blossom into the best people you can both possibly be.

APRIL 24TH

you will mean something different to everyone you come across in this lifetime, but make sure you don't lose sight of what you mean to yourself, because that's where the true gold exists.

there is so much power in finding or creating a place of acceptance for yourself. quieting the noise from everything external and listening to your voice within, silencing the lies you tell yourself as a result of opinions that don't belong to you and raising the volume on your truth, placing perfectionism on a shelf and putting your flaws unapologetically on a pedestal. when you're authentically being yourself, many will be confused by your essence, intimidated by your evolution, and even indifferent to who you are, but you can never change how they perceive you. *see their misunderstandings of you as the signs you've always needed to find more love for yourself than they could ever give you,* see them as signs to return back home to yourself, where you can strengthen and thicken the true opinion you should have of you.

APRIL 25TH

be careful not to drown yourself in waters filled with other people's problems.

it isn't your duty to fix anyone else's brokenness, it isn't your duty to restore people to their default settings, it isn't your duty to save anyone unwilling to find healing for themselves. your peace of mind is not worth sabotaging for people who are unwilling to hold themselves accountable, your boundaries are not worth breaking for situations that dissolve your true essence, your growth is not worth abandoning for things that fail to pour back into you. you can show compassion, softness, and love without adopting energy that doesn't belong to you—*sometimes the best way to help people heal is to let them take responsibility for their own wounds* instead of trying to wrap bandages over what they should be tending to themselves.

APRIL 26TH

trying to force something to click
won't help you find it any quicker.

it's so important to trust in exactly where you are even if you think you are deserving of much more, trust in the unknown even when your path is blurry and unclear, trust in your vision even when the destination is nowhere in sight. sometimes we fuel our intentions with fear and doubt, letting impatience take the wheel instead of letting divine timing drive us to where we need to be and where growth exists. the resistance you feel when something you want isn't going your way is usually an indication that what you're holding on to needs to be released; only then can something that speaks directly to your soul take its place. find acceptance for what can't be changed, and hold faith in what seems inescapable. *there are lessons to be learned in everything you go through, and there's a light at the end of the tunnel even when you can't see it.*

APRIL 27TH

trying to be strong all the time becomes exhausting.

strength is beautiful, but it was never meant to be worn like armor every single day. when you force yourself to be unshakable, you deny yourself the softness that makes you human. strength without rest turns into depletion. strength without vulnerability turns into isolation. you are allowed to collapse into yourself when you need to. you are allowed to admit that the weight is heavy, that the silence is loud, that the tears need somewhere to fall. this does not make you weak; it makes you honest, and honesty with yourself is the purest form of strength you will ever carry. rest does not erase resilience. *allowing yourself to be seen in your fragility does not cancel out your power.* the world has tricked you into thinking you have to hold it all together to be worthy of respect, but your wholeness is not measured by your ability to endure without breaking; it is measured by your courage to break when you must. you are human before you are anything else. let that truth give you permission to be soft, to be still, and to be tender with yourself. strength will return when it needs to, but for now, it is enough to simply *be.*

APRIL 28TH

you must leave some people in the past until they work on themselves. only then can they meet you where you are presently. you do this not out of malice or self-righteousness but because *you've worked too hard on yourself to take steps back in your growth* just so they can catch up to you.

APRIL 29TH

regret grows heavy when you carry it for too long.

regret was never meant to be carried as far as you've carried it. yet so often we strap it to our backs as if it is a part of who we are. we walk with it into every new season, unpack it in every new relationship, and convince ourselves that without it, we would lose our identity. but regret is not identity; it is weight, and weight is only useful if it teaches, not if it chains. *there comes a time when holding on to what you "should have done" begins to rob you of what you can still do.* forgiveness—not just toward others but toward yourself—is the lighter choice. forgive the version of you who didn't know better, who acted out of fear, who chose comfort over courage. that version of you was still learning. that version of you still deserves grace. the journey ahead asks for space. it asks for lighter steps, freer arms, a heart that can move without dragging the past behind it. let regret go. let forgiveness take its place. pack only what reminds you of your resilience, not your mistakes.

APRIL 30TH

who you are becoming will scare a lot of people who were too comfortable with who you used to be; it will frighten a lot of people afraid of heights to watch you ascend; it will intimidate a lot of people who viewed you as a comfort zone. continue to come into your own *unapologetically.*

midsummer.

MAY

protect my intentions.
hand me cups of awareness so
i may gravitate toward what is
meant for me, and fill my bones
with foresight so i may navigate
from what isn't. subdue my fears
so i can hear intuition more
clearly and so i can love myself
unapologetically. soak me in light.

MAY 1ST

any stage of your journey can be the catalyst for the life you want to live.

it's not too late to be whoever you want to be. it's not too late to start new goals for yourself. it's not too late to activate your dreams. it's not too late to begin the transformation you want to see. it's not too late to start viewing yourself in a better light. it's not too late to start watering your endeavors with the energy they deserve. it's not too late to start appreciating yourself where others have failed to. it's not too late to redirect your warmth inward. it's not too late to start choosing you. *your new era begins whenever you want it to,* however you want it to. you're right on time, right where you need to be; your intentions are the seeds that sprout it all.

MAY 2ND

reclaiming your magic will be a lonely path to walk at times because only you will truly know what you had to go through to obtain the formula to your freedom, only you will truly know how hard you've had to fight to find a way back home to yourself, only you will truly know the pain you've had to endure to heal the wounds that nobody else sees.

MAY 3RD

love yourself fully
so you can remain whole
without sacrificing parts of who you are
whenever you pour into them.

the amount of work you've put in or continue to put into yourself will always determine the quality of the relationships and friendships you attract. the amount of work you've put in or continue to put into yourself will also determine what you put up with and what you choose not to tolerate. *everything begins with you.* you are home base, the genesis, the origin. everything begins with your intentions, how you water them, how you nurture them; the universe reflects what you put in by bringing you closer to those who have looked at themselves as deeply as you've looked at yourself.

MAY 4TH

the book you once were
will become outdated and require you to rewrite yourself several times.
expand yourself into every new page.

you're always a work in progress, but you consist of infinite possibilities; there's always much more for you to discover at every stage of your metamorphosis. don't be too hard on yourself for chapters you're still stuck on or seasons that are going slower than you'd like. you haven't even begun to scratch the surface when it comes to your potential, and that's something to find excitement and solace in.

MAY 5TH

there is movement in becoming comfortable with stillness.

we are taught to glorify motion, to believe that if we are not running, producing, or chasing, we are somehow falling behind. but there is a different kind of growth that happens in stillness. it is not the absence of progress; it is the grounding of it. it is where your roots deepen, where your spirit regathers, where your clarity has space to speak. *even flowers, radiant as they are, cannot flourish if they are uprooted too often.* they bloom because they allow themselves to stay. there is a discipline in learning to rest, to breathe, to exist without rushing through the motions, and there is power in realizing that your life does not lose value when it slows down. some of the most profound shifts happen when you are still enough to notice them. so honor the pauses. let yourself be rooted long enough to absorb what you need. the world will try to tell you that stillness is wasted time, but stillness is where you remember who you are and where you quietly prepare for the next season of bloom.

MAY 6TH

it's the ones who give you the space to be yourself
who deserve to experience you at your fullest bloom.

the ones who create a space where you can breathe and express your deepest truths without fear of judgment. the ones who make you feel free enough to laugh, cry, dream, and simply exist. the ones who honor your individuality and encourage your growth. the ones who make you feel safe enough to see there is no need to wear masks or put up walls. the ones you can show up to as your raw, unfiltered self, knowing you are accepted and loved. these are the rare connections that understand the value of authenticity. your real community will always encourage you to be the fullest, most vibrant version of yourself. in giving you the freedom to be you, they give you the greatest gift of all: *the permission to live in your magic.*

MAY 7TH

allow whoever outgrows you to do so with no judgment or bitterness.

some people aren't meant to stay around for your entire journey; they are written into only a few chapters of your story before their role comes to an eventual end. the beauty of their presence is not measured by its length but by the lessons it leaves behind. when someone outgrows you, or when you outgrow them, it does not have to be seen as betrayal. it is simply growth doing what growth does—redirecting, reshaping, creating distance where alignment no longer lives. holding on too tightly to what has already served its purpose only creates more pain. gratitude is the softer way forward. gratitude for the moments shared, for the wisdom exchanged, for the role they played in helping you step closer to yourself. you don't have to curse the ending to honor the significance of the middle. release them with peace. let them walk their path without bitterness weighing on yours. understand that *every exit is also an entrance into deeper clarity,* into new connections, and into the next stage of your becoming. the ones who are meant to stay will grow with you. the ones who leave create space for what is next. both are gifts, and both deserve your thanks.

MAY 8TH

grief is as vast as the sea.
sometimes the waves are violent,
sometimes the waves are gentle,
but eventually you learn how to swim in it when it comes and goes.

time doesn't heal grief; you just learn how to carry it better with each day. it's like placing a heavy rock in a backpack and taking it with you everywhere you go—you may not see it until you open the bag, but you'll always feel it weighing you down. grief doesn't have a finish line; it's a never-ending marathon filled with echoes of sorrow. it's a road filled with different turns and hurdles that will require you to reroute your pain into places with growth, a path with different bumps and obstacles that will require you to redirect your sadness toward places with the potential for happiness. grief is a journey, a long expedition of emotions, an exploration of aching, a voyage of trying to understand emptiness. but allow it to take you on this trip, allow it to serve as a reminder that no matter how hard you may try to trick the mind, the heart always remembers, and maybe there's a reason for that. maybe by holding a space of gratitude for everything lost and the memories that remain, the beauty in grief can finally be found.

MAY 9TH

stay true to you; the worst promises that can ever be broken are the ones you make to yourself.

the most deafening silence comes from promises that you make to yourself, in the silent contracts that are signed in the solitude of your own heart. breaking a promise to a loved one might be hard to bear, a tearful conversation, a strained relationship, but *breaking a promise to yourself chips away at the core of your self-respect.* it erodes your trust in your own voice, it leaves a hollowness that rings loudly in your quiet moments. honor the quiet pacts you forge with your inner self, the commitments you make that no one else knows about; breaking them is like denying yourself the chance to become the person you were always meant to be.

MAY 10TH

you hand the key to your life to so many people,
then wonder why your happiness is misplaced when you're looking for it.

the key to your life isn't meant to be a token exchanged casually. it's a sacred trust, a responsibility that should be given only to those who have earned it, people who understand the delicate mechanisms of your heart like skilled locksmiths, people who possess the emotional intelligence to navigate your vulnerabilities with care and the strength to offer support without manipulating you. the world is filled with people who would snatch the key given the chance, who are eager to control your narrative, quick to steal your sparkle, open to exploiting your vulnerabilities for their own gain. so discern carefully; once the vault is unlocked, retrieving the key becomes an act of courage and a test of your boundaries. cultivate more self-awareness, understand your values, your dreams, and the direction you want your life to take. this empowers you to choose wisely, to recognize those who align with your vision and those who respect your right to navigate your own path. hold on to the key to your life tightly; *everyone you let through the door has the power to shift your happiness.*

MAY 11TH

some energy is too expensive to invest in.

better to let go and continue living your life than to hold on to the hope of something highly improbable happening; better to release yourself from what is unlikely to come to fruition than let it continue to steal your peace. some people will never truly understand how deeply their actions have affected you, even when you've made it clear, but internalizing and holding on to what they've done will only eat away at your happiness slowly. learn to *release yourself from the things that can't be changed* so you can find and attract new levels of tranquility.

MAY 12TH

planting yourself in other people's gardens
may help you grow temporarily,
but only in ways that they want you to.

it is easy to lose yourself when you are constantly searching for belonging in other people's spaces. you bend, you shrink, you adjust, trying to fit the shape of the soil they have prepared for you. and yes, you may grow there, but only in the directions they allow, only in ways that keep them comfortable. true growth requires your own ground. your own sunlight. your own rhythm. when you depend on someone else's garden to nourish you, you risk mistaking control for care. but the truth is, you carry your own seeds. you carry your own roots. you are not meant to be ornamental in someone else's landscape—*you are meant to bloom fully in your own space.* plant yourself where your spirit has room to stretch, where your growth isn't dictated but honored, where your becoming isn't limited by someone else's design, because flourishing borrowed from other people will always be conditional, but flourishing born from your own ground will always be free.

MAY 13TH

never let the importance of your dreams
be diminished by anyone
who doesn't have the courage to live out their own.

your dreams are sacred. they were whispered to your spirit for a reason, entrusted to you and no one else. not everyone will understand them, not everyone will support them, and many will try to shrink them—sometimes out of fear, sometimes out of envy, sometimes simply because they never found the strength to pursue their own. but their hesitation is not your burden. their doubt is not your reflection. often people project their limits on to you because it is easier to criticize what you're building than to face the emptiness of what they never started. you cannot let anyone's fear dilute your fire. if you allow them to diminish your vision, you inherit their limitations; if you continue to honor your calling, you inherit your freedom. the choice is always yours. walk boldly with your dreams, even if you walk alone. *trust that what was planted within you is not by accident.* the people who are meant to journey with you will not ask you to shrink; they will water the seed with you, and if no one else believes, believe anyway. your courage to live your dream is the very thing that will separate you from those who only ever spoke of theirs.

MAY 14TH

you are a rare specimen
divinely made
beautifully unique
they may try to replicate your blueprint
but *nothing about your spirit can be imitated*

MAY 15TH

your tenderness is a weapon.
after all the wars you've fought that no one knew about,
here you are,
still soft,
still *full of love.*

MAY 16TH

birth your ideas freely.

your ideas are the children of your spirit—sacred, delicate, unique, and born from the deepest parts of you. they deserve to breathe, to stretch, to take form in the world without shame, but understand: not every ear that listens is a safe place. not every smile in your audience is sincere. some people wait in your presence not to celebrate your blessings but to study them, to doubt them, even to dismantle them. this is why discernment matters. you do not have to silence your creativity, but you do have to protect it. not all soil is good soil, and not all hands know how to nurture what you've brought forth. some will love what you create because it reflects their own light, and others will resent it because it reminds them of what they've neglected within themselves. share wisely. move carefully. let your ideas grow roots within you before placing them in someone else's care. learn the difference between those who cheer out of genuine support and those who only clap loud enough to disguise their envy. and through it all, never stop birthing. never stop bringing your visions to life, because *your purpose is not dependent on their intentions—it is dependent on your courage to keep creating,* even when the room contains both love and resistance.

MAY 17TH

seasonal connections still have something to teach you
some people come into our lives to cool our concerns
some people come into our lives to help us bloom
some people come into our lives to keep us
warm during our coldest phases
and others come into our lives simply to teach
us that even if we shed our leaves
we can always re-create ourselves as many times as we need

—winter, spring, summer, fall

MAY 18TH

i am in sync with the universe even when i don't think i am.
i am on time to my destination even when i think i'm running late.

trust the timing of everything that is happening or not happening in your life, trust the sequence in which things are stalling or unfolding, trust the ways in which the waves are crashing or flowing. *everything has its season, and just as rivers flow effortlessly, so, too, must you with the currents of your journey.* surrender gently, and you will find that everything is perfectly in alignment, just as it is meant to be.

MAY 19TH

give yourself room to make mistakes
to *fail beautifully*
to be imperfect in your process
give yourself room to find lessons in everything
that hasn't gone the way you wanted

MAY 20TH

you'll be too much for some and too little for others,
but you are not required to be anyone else's definition of "enough."

it's a bitter truth to swallow that you will never be enough for certain people, but you free yourself when you learn to accept it. you release the need for validation from those who cannot give it, you reclaim your power, your peace, your pride. *let go of the need to be everything to everyone, and be everything you can be to yourself.* you will always be enough for the right people—the ones who see your heart, the ones who understand your soul, the ones who walk beside you on both sunny days and rainy nights. these are your people. hold them close, and let their love remind you of your own inherent value. in the end, you are the only one who needs to believe in your adequateness. stand tall in your self-worth, and find comfort in knowing that you are more than enough for those who matter most.

MAY 21ST

your identity is not rooted in what people used to know about you
it is not a composition of everything people
remember about you from the past
it is about the present
the way you flow in the current
who are you now?

MAY 22ND

to be loved for who you are now,
this is where the magic happens.

there is a different kind of freedom in being loved for who you are right now. not for who you might become, not for the version of you that exists only in someone else's imagination, but for the raw, unpolished, present you. so often, people fall in love with potential. they build castles in their minds about who you could be and then hold you hostage to their vision. they confuse their projections with love, and you end up carrying the burden of performing for a future you never promised, but *real love does not demand that you fast-forward your becoming.* real love honors your current chapter while still holding space for the chapters to come. it sees your flaws and calls them human. it sees your wounds and calls them worthy of care. it sees your dreams but does not rush you into them just to satisfy its own fantasy.

MAY 23RD

if you rush to your destination, think about all the beautiful things you'll miss along the way. think about all the untapped magic that will evade you because you moved quicker than you needed to.

—*slow down*

MAY 24TH

there are people who live only to dig out the resources that exist within you because they are too lazy to discover any gold that exists within themselves. you are not obligated to stay where anyone tries to excavate your self-worth for their own selfish purposes.

MAY 25TH

maturing is realizing that *truth is not always happy*
it's not always pleasant
it's not always sweet
it's not always easy
it's not always the way that you want it to look

MAY 26TH

i hope you learn to heal the parts of you that
feel guilty whenever you press pause
the parts of you that ache whenever you try to take a break
the parts of you still learning that *rest is also a necessity*

MAY 27TH

you're a work in progress and always under divine construction.

becoming yourself is not a gentle process. it requires demolition. it requires letting go of habits, beliefs, and versions of you that once felt permanent but no longer serve the life you are trying to create. it can feel like loss, but it is really rebuilding. you are always under construction, always being reshaped, refined, renewed. the breaking is never a punishment; it is preparation. whenever something falls apart, and every time an old layer is stripped away, you are being given space to build something authentic, something much sturdier, something more aligned with the person you are becoming. the timing, the lessons, and the tearing down are not accidents: they're divine work. even the moments that feel like ruin are part of the blueprint. you are not being reduced; you are being redesigned. trust that what feels like destruction is really foundation building. the life you long for is not built overnight; it is built brick by brick, release by release, surrender by surrender, and one day, when the dust clears, you'll see it: a version of yourself that could exist only because you were willing to let the old walls fall.

MAY 28TH

darkness has much to teach you, too.

we often treat darkness like an enemy. something to escape, something to fear, something to endure until light returns, but darkness is not always here to harm you. sometimes it arrives as a teacher. sometimes it comes to strip away the noise of the world so that you can finally hear the voice within. when the lights are off, there is nothing left to distract you; no illusions to hide behind, no performances to maintain, just you, your silence, and the thoughts you've been running from. it is in these moments that truth rises, the truths that daylight buries under busyness, under company, under distractions. darkness forces you to sit with yourself, to face the corners of your spirit you'd rather avoid. it is uncomfortable, but within that heaviness lives clarity, within that silence lives answers. don't rush through the dark seasons. don't curse them as wasted time; allow them to do their work, to sharpen your vision, to deepen your understanding, because *the lessons you learn in the dark will guide you when the light returns.* and when the light returns, you'll see more clearly, love more deeply, and walk more intentionally because the darkness taught you how.

MAY 29TH

not everything that leaves needs to be replaced.

we are conditioned to fill every gap, to rush into replacing whatever leaves us, whether it's a relationship, a role, a season, or a piece of identity we've outgrown. silence feels uncomfortable, emptiness feels unbearable, but not everything that exits in your life is meant to be replaced. *sometimes loss is an invitation not to seek newness outside of yourself but to deepen your presence within.* sometimes the space that opens up is not a void but a doorway for you to step into yourself more fully, to reclaim the energy you once poured outward, to expand in ways you could not when you were crowded by what no longer fit. you do not always need someone else to take up the room. you do not always need a new dream, a new distraction, or a new purpose to immediately step into. you are allowed to let the emptiness breathe, to let it hold you, to let it remind you that your own presence can be enough. the absence you feel is not always a loss; sometimes it is an offering. sometimes it is your guides telling you, *here is space—fill it with more of you.*

MAY 30TH

when you look in the mirror
do you see you
or who the world is asking you to be?

—necessary questions

MAY 31ST

uncuff yourself from any guilt that says that you're asking for too much.

wanting more does not make you ungrateful. it does not make you greedy. it simply means that the vision within you refuses to settle for a life that doesn't honor its fullness. yet, so often, guilt slips in, telling you that you should be satisfied with less, that you are selfish for desiring more peace, more love, more abundance, more freedom. but guilt is a chain, not a compass. it keeps you tied to a version of yourself that is too small, too afraid, too dependent on the approval of others. the truth is, asking for more is not arrogance—it is alignment. it is your soul tugging you closer to what you were always meant to experience. uncuff yourself from that guilt. release the belief that your dreams are "too much" or that your desires are unreasonable. what is unreasonable is silencing the pull in your spirit just to remain palatable for others. you are allowed to stretch. you are allowed to reach. you are allowed to step into spaces that honor the expanse of who you are. wanting more has never been a crime; it is merely evidence that you are aware enough to imagine something greater for yourself.

JUNE

aid in my ascension. let the things
i plant come to fruition and
give wings to the things that are
meant for me. open doors for
the things i need, and close them
on what is no longer conducive.
let the love i have for myself
guide me back whenever
i forget where home is.

JUNE 1ST

punishing yourself for how your younger self operated won't make flowers grow from those mistakes. being harsh on yourself for how older versions of you mishandled certain situations won't strengthen your roots. *forgive yourself for what you did when you didn't know better.* that's how you make seeds sprout in barren soil.

JUNE 2ND

pain can either raise or lower your standards.

pain has a way of reshaping you. sometimes it softens you into someone wiser, someone clearer, someone unwilling to settle for less than what your heart deserves, and sometimes, if you're not careful, it can lower the bar, convincing you to accept less, to tolerate mistreatment, to shrink your desires just to avoid being hurt again. this is the delicate balance of healing. when you begin that journey, you have to choose which direction pain will take you. will it raise your standards, reminding you of what you should never allow back into your life? or will it weigh you down, teaching you to expect disappointment, to surrender to cycles that don't honor your worth? your pain is not just something to survive; it is something to learn from. let it be a teacher that builds your boundaries, not a thief that steals your vision. *let it be the lesson that sharpens your discernment, not the scar convincing you that love and joy are too dangerous to pursue.* healing is not about erasing the pain; it's about choosing what the pain creates in you. raise the bar. keep it high. let your wounds remind you not of how fragile you are but of how sacred you are.

JUNE 3RD

giving up your authenticity for who the world wants or expects you to be is never a fair trade.

there is no reward worth the price of abandoning yourself. the world will try to convince you that blending in is safer, that fitting their image of you will make life easier, but what use is being loved for a version of you that doesn't even exist? authenticity is not always applauded, but it is always freeing. every time you choose to honor who you really are, you take your power back. every time you silence yourself to please others, you hand that power away. the truth is, losing people because you were yourself will never hurt as much as losing yourself because you wanted to keep people. you were not created to be a replica of the world's expectations; you were created to stand in your own design, to breathe in your own rhythm, to shine in your own light. anything less is not living; it's performing, and *life is too sacred to be lived on a stage.*

JUNE 4TH

some people come into our lives and stop the music completely; some come into our lives and the music continues to play; others come into our lives and add more drums, strings, and layers to what already existed to create a new melody that feels more like home.

JUNE 5TH

being the cycle breaker can be daunting.
you're the one, out of everyone who came before you,
who understands the importance of changing the generational course.
but being the cycle breaker can also be exciting if you allow it to be.
you're the one to start a new era of healthier and
better patterns for generations to come.

JUNE 6TH

you will understand some people more than they make an effort to understand you.

not every connection will feel balanced. sometimes you will love more, give more, listen more, and carry more than the other person is willing or able to offer in return. you will hold their silence with compassion while they mishandle your words. you will study their storms while they barely glance at your skies. it is a bitter truth that *your depth will not always be met with depth,* that your effort will not always be reciprocated, and if you are not careful, you will start to believe this imbalance is a reflection of your worth. not everyone was meant to meet you where you stand, not everyone was taught to love with the same tenderness you carry. some people will only ever taste the surface of who you are because they cannot handle the oceans within you. so let it be. do not dim your understanding to match their lack of it, do not lower your care to make the imbalance less noticeable. keep being you, even if it means loving people more than they love you. but also, learn when to step back, when to protect your energy, when to stop pouring into cups that refuse to fill yours, because in the end, your capacity to understand others is a gift, and you must save enough of that gift to also understand, honor, and protect yourself.

JUNE 7TH

don't become the monster or ghost in your own story by betraying who you are.

betraying yourself is the quickest way to disappear from your own story. anytime you lower the volume on your truth to make someone else comfortable, you start fading into the background of your own life. every time you shrink your flame so that others don't have to confront their shadows, you trade your freedom for their comfort, but you were never born to be the ghost of yourself, haunting a life that doesn't even reflect who you are. you were never created to play the villain in your own narrative, wearing masks just to protect people from seeing what they refuse to face within themselves. real love, real connection, will never ask you to abandon yourself. it will never require you to carve away pieces of your identity just to be "easier to love." so hold on to your truth with both hands. stand firm in your reflection. *if your light unsettles someone, let them deal with their discomfort;* it is not your job to make it easier for them to avoid their own mirror. your only responsibility is to remain whole, to remain present, to remain you.

JUNE 8TH

i am getting to where i need to be.

the journey will rarely look the way you imagined it. the map you drew in your mind may not match the one life hands you. sometimes you will take detours you never planned for, sometimes you will walk through valleys you never thought you'd enter, and sometimes the timeline will stretch longer than your patience would prefer, but none of that means you are lost. none of that means you are behind. it only means the path is shaping you as much as the destination is calling you. the delays, the reroutes, the pauses, they are all parts of the preparation. you are still moving forward, even when it doesn't feel like it; you are still being led, even when the steps are unclear, and every twist in the road is proof that you are being guided, not abandoned. trust that you are arriving. trust that *divine timing bends not to your expectations but to your growth.* you will get to where you are meant to be, and when you arrive, you will see why it couldn't have happened any other way.

JUNE 9TH

sometimes you have to leave the fabric of who you were
to stitch yourself into a newer timeline
more fitting of the clothing you're growing into.

you're human. growing attached to things, memories, and people is normal, but if you're ever asked to release what doesn't want to stay, you owe it to yourself to let go so you can open up more pathways for your growth. *believe that everything that leaves is only creating more space for better,* believe that everything that leaves has something to teach you, believe that everything that leaves is only helping you to see yourself more clearly. *allow it. let it outgrow you.*

JUNE 10TH

your healing will never start, sound, feel, or end like anyone else's.

we often get so caught up in the frustration of the healing process that we forget there isn't a linear or specific way it's supposed to go, there isn't a particular way it's supposed to unfold or take effect, there isn't a fixed way it's supposed to feel or manifest. give yourself grace through everything you're experiencing and everything you've been through. *no path back to yourself will ever be straightforward,* but no matter how long it takes and no matter how frustrating it can be, the road back home will always be worth it.

JUNE 11TH

imagine worrying about what someone who doesn't know themselves thinks about you?

so much of the weight you carry comes from opinions that were never meant to define you. people who haven't even sat with their own reflection will try to speak into yours, people who run from their own truth will try to edit yours. for too long you've let voices that don't even know themselves shape how you see yourself, but *why hand over your peace to those still searching for their own?* why let someone lost in their own maze dictate how you walk your path? not every opinion is worth holding, not every judgment deserves space in your spirit. your worth was never meant to be measured by someone else's confusion. it was meant to be lived, owned, and carried by you, unapologetically. free yourself from the need to be understood by those who have not yet understood themselves. stand tall in who you are. be rooted in your truth, and let the noise of unsteady voices pass by you like background static, heard but never listened to.

JUNE 12TH

are you dwelling on the pain because you can't let it go,
or are you dwelling on the pain because it's all you know?

—*release*

JUNE 13TH

endings can be beautifully auspicious.

trust that everything that has ended or is currently ending for you right now is only paving the way to something much better. *there is nothing coincidental about the timing when something exits your life;* there is nothing coincidental about the phase in which people show you their true selves; there is nothing coincidental about chapters finally closing in books you thought would never end. honor what chooses not to stay so you can welcome in what is meant for you; *anything that you weren't able to keep hold of was never for you to begin with.*

JUNE 14TH

you cannot write yourself into someone else's story and save them from their plight.

it's in the struggle, in the quiet battles fought in the shadows, that resilience is born. you might want to swoop in for those you love and care about, cape flowing, heart open, ready to rescue them, but sometimes the most loving thing you can do is take a step back, to watch from the sidelines, knowing that the power to rise has always been within them. they might stumble, but in those falls, they may also find their wings. in those stumbles, they may finally learn how to navigate the storms within. in the end, it's not about being saved; it's about discovering that they were never broken, just bending. *it's about realizing that they had the strength all along to save themselves.* you can be their guiding star, their quiet encouragement, their source of belief, but sometimes the most heroic thing you could ever do is let them be the savior in their own story.

JUNE 15TH

misery is one of the worst places to make a home.
people walk in and can sense the sadness without you saying a word.
people walk out with some of your essence
still lingering in their energy field.
it is a place that must be inhabited only temporarily
while you learn to move into spaces with more love.

JUNE 16TH

anger has its lessons, but when you hold on to it for too long, it starts to poison you.

anger comes to remind you of your boundaries. it arrives to show you what hurts, what you will no longer tolerate, what needs to change, but anger was never meant to move in with you. it is a guest, not a resident, and when you let it linger too long, it begins to shape your voice, your choices, and your energy until you no longer recognize yourself. your power isn't found in staying angry; it's found in transforming it, in letting the fire burn long enough to give you clarity but not so long that it burns down everything you've built. anger can point you toward the truth, but peace is what allows you to embody it. don't let anger cloud your brilliance. don't let it dim the softness, the love, the magic that makes you who you are. it is one thing to acknowledge your hurt; it is another to live in it. choose release. choose alignment. choose to keep your hands free so you can create instead of clenched so tightly around what wounded you. your essence was never designed to survive in the poison of resentment; *your essence was meant to thrive in the freedom of letting go.*

JUNE 17TH

the most selfless kind of love will always
make your presence feel valued
while simultaneously reminding you
that you belong to yourself.

the purest love has no intention of keeping you chained; it lifts you like a soaring kite, tethered by trust but free to explore the depths of the entire sky. it allows you to maintain your individuality, your passions, and your dreams while celebrating the joy of flying together. true love doesn't demand ownership; it fosters independence. it empowers you to explore your own path, knowing that your partner will be there to support you, not clip your wings. it celebrates your individual triumphs and offers a safe space to return to, *a space where your authentic self can breathe freely* when the pressures of the world threaten to suffocate you.

JUNE 18TH

when you acknowledge your pain, it becomes less intimidating and less of a giant.

pain grows louder the more you run from it. it becomes this shadow that follows you into every room, stretching bigger the more you refuse to turn and face it, but when you pause, when you give it a name, when you acknowledge it, the shadow shrinks. it no longer towers over you. it becomes something you can hold, examine, and eventually release. *pain was never meant to be a life sentence; it was meant to be a teacher.* one that only quiets down once you let it speak. when you finally lean in, you realize it's not here to destroy you; it's here to show you where the healing must begin.

JUNE 19TH

you will never find love where you are being taken for granted.
you will never find acceptance where there is
commitment to misconstrue your intent.
you will never find light in rooms that block out the windows to your soul.

love doesn't dwell in the shadows of neglect or in the shell of empty promises. it doesn't thrive where your worth is questioned, it doesn't breathe where your heart is overlooked or where your soul is left wanting. it recognizes you, cherishes your essence, and celebrates your presence. you find it in the eyes that see you, in the arms that hold you, in the words that uplift you, and in the *intentions that match the lyrics in your soul's playlist.* anything else that makes you feel unaccepted is only showing you what you shouldn't settle for.

JUNE 20TH

you are not who you were last year
or who you were last month,
you are not who you were last week
or who you were yesterday.
you are always evolving.
how could you ever be defined?

JUNE 21ST

how anyone feels about you will always be secondary to how you feel about yourself.

how you choose yourself will determine how you unlock the doors to every other part of your life. things start to shift when you embrace yourself as the catalyst needed for things to start changing within you and around you instead of waiting on someone or something to provide that spark. too many times we become overly reliant on external factors to determine how things in our lives should look or how we should carry ourselves, but you have always been the key, carved specifically for your journey, infused with energy fitting of all the hard work you've put into yourself, made with an abundance of love that already exists within you. accept yourself in your entirety, the good, the imperfect, the work in progress, the potential; accept yourself first and the universe will always find different ways of holding your intentions closely.

JUNE 22ND

your lane is a unique one
it belongs to you and you alone
constantly comparing your path to everyone else's
takes away from the magic your footprints
are leaving in your own journey

JUNE 23RD

how you reclaim yourself will feel foreign to those yet to find a home within themselves.

your seclusion won't always be accepted, your solitude won't always be understood, your reclusiveness won't always be comprehended. sometimes your need for space will be met with false opinions or misguided ideas, but never attach guilt to the moments when you require time away from the noise or distractions to recharge your sense of self. sometimes it will take isolation for you to see yourself clearly again, sometimes it will take distance for you to claim yourself again, sometimes it will take separation for you to find yourself again; *how it looks when you're learning how to love yourself again is no one's business but your own.*

JUNE 24TH

you can walk away and still find your footing elsewhere
you can walk away and still grow elsewhere
you can walk away and still find happiness elsewhere
you can walk away and still find you

JUNE 25TH

keeping some of you to yourself is how you protect your energy
keeping some of you to yourself is how you hold on to your magic.

keep some of you to you; protect your energy like the precious gift it is. not everyone is meant to touch the deepest parts of you, to experience the sacred space you hold, to access the core of your being. there's power in holding on to pieces of yourself and not giving everything away. reserve some of your sweetness for you, enjoy the solace of your own company, let the world see your light, but allow the flames to always burn for yourself first. in a world that often asks for more and demands your attention by pulling at your essence, find the courage to say no and the bravery to draw boundaries that honor your spirit; *find the love to guard your magic.*

JUNE 26TH

reconciliation without actionable change or accountability is just self-sabotage.

words can be beautiful, but beauty without substance is a mirage. apologies can sound poetic, and promises can sound convincing, but if nothing shifts in behavior and no effort is made to repair what was broken, then all you are holding on to is an echo. forgiveness is not about returning to the same cycle that hurt you. reconciliation without action is just a performance, a way of keeping you tethered to hope while nothing truly changes, and if you accept that performance long enough, you end up betraying yourself, not because of what they did but because of what you allowed. *love should not be a trap wrapped in pretty language.* love should not be about constantly giving someone the benefit of the doubt when their actions prove they deserve otherwise. it should be about honesty, accountability, and growth. so guard your heart against empty gestures. listen beyond the words. watch how consistently someone chooses you in the everyday moments and not just when they are afraid to lose you, because your peace deserves more than rehearsed speeches. it deserves action, it deserves truth. it deserves someone who builds, not someone who only speaks of building.

JUNE 27TH

silence will speak better for you on some days, and that's okay.

there are some days when silence will speak louder than any words you can find. it carries your weight without asking for explanation. it holds your storms without needing to justify them. not every feeling is meant for translation. *not every thought has a dialect that fits neatly into sentences.* forcing it too soon can twist its meaning or, worse, dilute its power. learning to sit with yourself in quiet is a form of self-respect. it tells the world, and yourself, that your inner world is sacred, that your emotions are allowed to exist fully, even without a voice. so, in the places where language fails you, allow silence to do the work instead. let it protect what cannot be spoken yet; you are still whole, still seen, and still valid in that stillness.

JUNE 28TH

there is a deep suffering that comes with
comparing your growth to everyone else's
your journey will be distinctive
allow it to bend
allow it to curve
allow it to take a unique shape all its own

JUNE 29TH

release the shame that comes with asking for help when you need it.

there is nothing wrong with seeking assistance. the world tells you to be unbreakable, to carry everything alone, to measure strength by how quietly you struggle, but strength is not immunity, resilience is not a shield against life's weight. asking for help does not make you less; it makes you honest, it makes you human. it reminds you that even the most capable hearts still need hands to hold, shoulders to lean on, voices to guide. release the guilt. release the fear that needing support is a flaw. it is an act of courage, an act of wisdom, an act of self-respect. to reach out is not surrender; it is participation in the world. it is recognition that you do not have to face everything alone and that, sometimes, allowing someone in is the strongest thing you can do.

JUNE 30TH

sometimes it will take more than just enforcing
or communicating boundaries for people to truly
understand how you want to be loved or treated.
sometimes it will mean removing yourself from situations that
aren't changing by *respecting yourself* enough to create distance.

JULY

show me the magic that exists
within. let me unearth buried
diamonds in my soul that
i've ignored in the past. let the
love i have for myself be so loud
that it silences unnecessary
opinions. allow truth to find
me even when the world
shuts its lights off.

JULY 1ST

their opinions of you aren't your concern.
what they think of you isn't something you can control.
the more time you spend trying to be liked
by people who already have their minds made up about you,
the more of your magic you give away.

JULY 2ND

when was the last time you applauded yourself for how far you've come?

when was the last time you clapped for yourself not because you reached the finish line but because you kept walking when the road was breaking beneath you? we forget that survival is a kind of magic, that choosing to rise every morning, even when yesterday was heavy, is an act of quiet heroism. we get so used to holding a magnifying glass over our mistakes, over the places we could have been sharper, faster, better, but what about the places where you were softer? where you offered yourself patience? where you stayed, even when leaving would have been easier? your journey isn't just measured by the milestones you've conquered; it's written in the moments when you refused to give up on yourself.

JULY 3RD

you will only get to experience this exact moment,
right now, once in your lifetime.

you will only get to touch this moment once. it will never repeat itself in the same way, with the same air, the same light, the same pulse of your heart. we spend so much of our days running after tomorrow, replaying yesterday, that we forget how rare *now* really is. this breath is not just oxygen; it is memory in the making, it is proof that you are still here, still becoming, still unfolding into someone you have not fully met yet. breathe it in. let the weight of gratitude sit on your chest, let it seep into your bones. this moment is a fragrance, fleeting and eternal at the same time. you will never smell it again, but if you slow down enough, you can carry its essence with you wherever you go. remember this scent; it belongs only to today.

JULY 4TH

hold yourself as tightly as the night holds fireworks,
and celebrate yourself every chance you get.

hold yourself without hesitation, without question, without fear of being too much. the sky never wonders if it is worthy of the light exploding inside it, it simply opens and receives. you, too, deserve to be received in that way. too often we wait for someone else's applause, someone else's recognition, forgetting that our spirit blooms best in the warmth of our own hands. you are both the spark and the celebration; you are both the flame and the witness. celebrate yourself loudly, quietly, in fragments, in full. celebrate the small victories that no one else sees. celebrate the way you've carried yourself through storms. celebrate the way you continue to rise, even when no one is watching. your life is a festival; don't wait for permission to dance beneath your own light.

JULY 5TH

things can change overnight,
things can change in an instant,
things can change in a heartbeat.
your world could be on the verge of a deep transformation.
don't give up now.

things rarely warn you before they change. the tide turns without a sound, the season shifts without asking permission, the heart learns how to bloom again in silence. one moment can undo years of waiting, one heartbeat can rewrite an entire story. *just because you can't see the transformation doesn't mean it isn't happening.* life is always rearranging itself for your becoming, even in the shadows, even in the quiet. so hold on, breathe through the doubt. don't walk away right before the miracle. you might be standing at the edge of a sunrise that will color your entire world differently.

JULY 6TH

living a life where you're constantly trying to prove other people wrong becomes draining and exhausting because it feeds only your ego; your soul still remains hungry.

falling into cycles of seeking validation from those who don't see your worth becomes an unending chase for approval you may never receive. you deserve more than that. you deserve to live freely, authentically, in tune with your own frequency, in line with your own truth. your worth isn't measured by how many doubters you can silence but by how deeply you embrace yourself. *it's not about proving anyone wrong; it's about proving yourself right.* Let your actions be driven by your own desires, not by the need to refute someone else's expectations or judgments. living for the approval of others is a game you can't win, a sea that drowns you beneath the waves, a flame that eventually burns you out.

JULY 7TH

holding on to expired versions of yourself only
blocks your pathways to growth
it only shuts your doors to new opportunities
it only obstructs your avenues to fresh beginnings
heal who you used to be so you can become who you need to be

JULY 8TH

you will never gain anything by consistently returning to places that put you on mute when your heart has much to say.

you will never grow in places that shrink you. you will never be fully seen in rooms that choose to dim your light. the heart is not meant to whisper forever; it was built to sing, to speak, to take up space without apology. returning to spaces that silence you is a slow betrayal of your own voice. every time you mute yourself to be accepted, you forget that acceptance without authenticity is just another form of abandonment. choose the rooms that reflect back your truth. choose the people who make your words feel like home. choose the spaces where your heart does not have to beg to be heard. you were not made to be background noise; *you were made to be magical music.*

JULY 9TH

if it starts to cloud your discernment, then maybe it just isn't for you,
that connection, that opportunity, that situation
if it begins to muddy your judgment,
wipe the dirt off your intentions and remove yourself from that energy.

JULY 10TH

the brutal truth is that *there are some people who won't deserve an explanation,* there are some people who won't be worth your words. your actions and your energy will have to show them exactly how you feel and get your point across even in silence, regardless of how painful or uncomfortable it may be.

JULY 11TH

i am constantly evolving and never obligated
to stay the same for anyone.

you've come too far to stop watering everything beautiful growing within you for anything or anyone that doesn't appreciate your progress or growth, you've come too far to halt who you're becoming to embody who the masses expect you to be. sometimes we get so lost in whether our "enough" is enough for other people, but *who we're enough for isn't as important as whether we think we're enough for ourselves.*

JULY 12TH

honor the friendships and connections that encourage you to be your authentic self but still see you even when you aren't seeing yourself fully. these are the connections that help you *maintain your magic* during your low phases.

JULY 13TH

be for you first, everyone else can wait.

the world will always pull at your time, your heart, your energy. people will always have needs, always have expectations, always ask for pieces of you. but before you hand yourself out, you have to make sure there is something whole left to give. being for yourself first is not selfish; it is survival. it is choosing to fill your own cup so you don't keep pouring from emptiness. it is listening to your own needs before they turn into silent resentment. it is protecting your peace so you can show up from a place of strength, not exhaustion. when you belong to yourself first, you love better. you give without bitterness. you help without losing yourself. you show up without abandoning your own needs, and the people who truly value you will never resent the boundaries that keep you whole. so pause. breathe. ask yourself what you need today. honor it. nourish it. love it. everyone else can wait a moment while you come home to yourself, because *if you lose you in the process of giving to others, there will be nothing left to give at all.*

JULY 14TH

you're blooming even in your uneventful moments.

it's not only in the spectacular and loud chapters that you are blooming; the quiet phases, the repetitive seasons, the moments that feel still and uneventful—those are equally sacred. *growth doesn't always come dressed in fireworks;* sometimes it arrives in silence, in patience, in the invisible shifts of your spirit. trust the slow phases. trust the boring chapters. they are teaching you how to hold yourself, how to water your roots when nothing seems to be blossoming. even when you can't see it, life is rearranging you, preparing you, softening you for what's ahead. growth is not always a sprint; sometimes it's a gentle unfolding of your magic.

JULY 15TH

being seen isn't everything.
it isn't always a telltale sign that you're felt or understood.
it isn't a full indication that those around you appreciate your essence.
seeing yourself is where the true magic is. *lean into it.*

JULY 16TH

make a habit of spending intentional time with yourself, away from the distractions, away from the noise, away from anything and anyone that pulls you away from you.

make a consistent habit of meeting yourself in stillness. step away from the screens, the chatter, the weight of expectation, and return to the sound of your own breath. there is wisdom in your silence, there is guidance in your solitude. when you strip away the noise, you begin to hear the language of your soul more clearly. when you set down the distractions, you remember how much you've carried, how much you've endured, how much of yourself you've left waiting for you. the world will always try to pull you in every direction, but *you belong to yourself first.* give yourself that time, give yourself that attention, give yourself that love.

JULY 17TH

allow your failed connections to make room for
everything that you should be attracting.
allow your failed connections to make space
for potential goodness to come.
allow your failed connections to open the door to people
better suited for the direction you're heading in.

JULY 18TH

you soothe your nervous system every time you choose to surrender instead of resisting in situations you don't have much control over.

peace begins where resistance ends; every time you loosen your grip on what you cannot change, you remind your nervous system that safety can be found in surrender. not every struggle is meant to be wrestled with, not every storm is asking for your fight. sometimes the bravest thing you can do is breathe, soften; sometimes the most courageous thing you can do is release the weight of control and trust the current to carry you where you're meant to go. surrender is not weakness; it is wisdom. it is the body remembering that it does not have to live in battle or survival mode all the time. when you surrender, you pour honey into the places inside you that are tired of bracing for impact.

JULY 19TH

breathe.
there is nothing ordinary about you
or the things you've gone through.
so why would anything
about your healing be, either?

JULY 20TH

you are a divine work in progress, an imperfect soul still constructing your ideal experience, an angel still trying to find its wings. *the masterpiece has always been you;* the universe is just waiting for you to realize it.

JULY 21ST

forgiveness doesn't solve everything, but it allows you to feel less attached to the hurt. it allows you to decrease the weight being placed on your soul. it allows you to *create more room to occupy with love.*

JULY 22ND

you deserve time to come into your own without being
rushed into becoming the finished article.
you deserve time to focus on you without fearing
the loss of connection or opportunity.
you deserve the patience to become a fuller you
without sacrificing parts of yourself.

JULY 23RD

you being you will be too bright for the wrong people.

how you celebrate yourself will confuse those who know only how to dim their own light. *how you choose yourself will overwhelm those who benefit from your self-abandonment,* and how you continue to be fully you will feel too bright for those who have grown comfortable in shadows. but remember, your joy was never meant to be filtered for easier digestion. your light was never meant to be dialed down to make others comfortable. you are not responsible for how others receive the wholeness of you. the right people will not be blinded by your brilliance; they will bask in it. the right people will not question your celebration; they will clap with you. the right people will not shrink from your choosing; they will honor it. be loud in your joy, be firm in your choosing, be unapologetic in your being; brightness is only "too much" for those who are not ready to see clearly.

JULY 24TH

the worst person you could ever go to war with is yourself.
show yourself compassion.
lay your weapons down.
you've injured yourself far too many times already.

it's so easy to fall into the habit of torturing yourself over things you did in your lowest phases or in situations where your weak moments got the better of you, but what you did when you weren't seeing yourself clearly doesn't deserve to have a permanent hold over your life, it doesn't deserve the power to control your story or narrative, it doesn't deserve to be a souvenir you hold on to as a reminder.
be gentle with yourself, exercise kindness throughout, and always remember: *you're doing the best you can.*

JULY 25TH

heading in the same direction with someone doesn't mean you'll ultimately end up at the same destination. *respect your unique path, and respect theirs.* there's beauty to be found in each unique experience, even if it sees you landing somewhere completely different from where you both imagined.

JULY 26TH

find gratitude for what you already have instead of worrying about what hasn't come yet.

gratitude is the anchor that keeps you steady when your mind wants to drift into fear of what hasn't arrived yet. it reminds you that even here, even now, you are surrounded by blessings you once prayed for. it is easy to live in the ache of absence, to measure your worth by what still hasn't shown up, but *there is peace in pausing long enough to notice the gifts already in your hands,* the love already in your life, the breath already moving through your body. gratitude isn't an indication of settling; it is simply a softening into the truth that you are already enough and that you already hold so much. from that place of fullness, the things you are waiting for have space to find you.

JULY 27TH

how you reclaim yourself will be more misunderstood than felt
it will confuse many people who were familiar
with older versions of you
but *how you choose to walk back into your own life*
is no one else's concern but your own

JULY 28TH

the misaligned routes you try to force open will always lead you to places that aren't meant for you.

the paths you have to force are not the ones that will carry you home. misaligned doors may open, but they will only lead you further away from yourself. forcing what isn't meant for you is a quiet way of abandoning your own alignment. life has a rhythm, and when you move with it, you'll find yourself guided to places that welcome you without resistance. the right opportunities will not demand that you twist yourself out of shape, the right people will not require you to beg for a seat at the table. not every room is yours to occupy, not every path is yours to walk, and that is the magic.

JULY 29TH

understand yourself so their misconceptions
of you don't become your reality.
understand yourself so their ideas of you don't become your own.
understand yourself so deeply that no matter
how much they misunderstand you,
your truth remains *impenetrable.*

JULY 30TH

there is nothing coincidental about the things unfolding in your life.

there is nothing coincidental about the way your life is moving. the shifts, the stillness, the detours, the delays—they are all parts of a rhythm bigger than you. not everything is meant to change at once, and not everything is meant to remain forever. the pendulum swings back and forth, teaching you balance. one side asks you to surrender, the other asks you to trust, and in between those swings, you are being stretched into patience, into resilience, into deeper faith in your own journey. *peace is found in knowing that whether life is in motion or in pause, you are still being guided to exactly where you need to be.*

JULY 31ST

letting go isn't easy when you've invested so much,
but your happiness also depreciates the
longer you hold on to what isn't for you.

your resistance is blocking your route to growth, your stubbornness is delaying your pathways to healing, your inflexibility is narrowing your lane to peace. it won't be easy to welcome in every single feeling that goes against the grain of your soul, but some things are not meant to be understood as much as they are meant to be accepted. *allow all the shifts that rock your world* so you can make space for what you deserve.

AUGUST

refine my energy. reignite the
love i have for myself, and
pour cold water on anything
or anyone that tries to take
that away. give me the patience
to ignore what i can't control
and the awareness to recognize
what i need to embrace.
coat my intentions in gold.

AUGUST 1ST

be the right person so you can see what the right people look like when they find you.

to see the right people, you must first become the right person. it's about feeding your soul, tending your spirit, and inviting your authentic self to the table. when you cultivate love within, you attract love that understands how deeply you've had to work on yourself, you attract love that meets you where you are instead of where you've been. when you walk in your truth, you become familiar with those walking in theirs. it's not about searching for the right people; it's about becoming the lighthouse that draws them near. your energy speaks before you do; let it speak of love, of growth, of realness. then the right people will not just find you; they'll recognize you, and in their hearts, you'll see a reflection of the beauty that exists within you.

AUGUST 2ND

no one will ever understand the depths of what
you've been through except you.
never let anyone who hasn't been in your seat take
the wheel and hijack your experience.

there will be plenty of times on your journey when conforming seems more comfortable than being honest, many situations in which passiveness appears more attractive than confrontation, several moments when appeasing egos will feel easier than prioritizing you, but the guilt for choosing yourself in these phases isn't your weight to sustain. not everyone will be able to understand all the actions you carry through or all the ideas you put in place as you try to find ways to tap into the highest version of yourself, but staying the course and *remaining loyal to your growth is how you respect your process.* shifting your energy back inward is how you rekindle your magic. may you find comfort in being you, even if being you is too bright for them to handle.

AUGUST 3RD

being who people want you to be instead of who you want to be is the quickest road to emptiness, exhaustion, and loneliness. no connection is worth investing in if it requires that you put on an act, *no space is worth occupying if you have to put a mask on to breathe,* no role is worth stepping into if it makes you feel like less of yourself.

AUGUST 4TH

your scars can feel ugly and hard to look at, but take pride in what you've healed from. the battles you fought gave you awareness that only few can dream of, and everything you've been through has given you the invaluable gift of *perspective.*

AUGUST 5TH

you were never falling apart.
all the pieces in your life are just being
rearranged so you can understand the bigger picture.

you were never falling apart, even on the days it felt like everything was slipping through your fingers. what you called breaking was really shifting. what you called crumbling was really clearing. the pieces of your life weren't leaving you; they were learning where they truly belonged. *sometimes life has to scatter the puzzle so you can stop forcing shapes that don't fit together.* sometimes the old arrangement has to be undone so you can finally see the bigger picture you were too close to notice. the job that ended, the love that left, the dream that dissolved—all of it was moving you out of what was too small for you. and yes, it hurt. it always hurts when life rearranges you. but one day, you will look back and realize the chaos was construction. the detours were redirection. the silence was a seed. nothing was wasted, not even the moments that made you doubt yourself. you were never falling apart—you were being rewritten. piece by piece, season by season, you were being put back together into someone fuller, someone stronger, someone finally able to carry the weight of the vision waiting for you. the bigger picture was never gone. it was just waiting for you to grow into the eyes that could see it.

AUGUST 6TH

learn to leave people in their comfort zone if their presence is forcing you to stay in yours. your growth is too important to abandon for anyone who promotes stagnancy on your journey because they are unwilling to put footsteps into their own.

AUGUST 7TH

the conversations and things you tell yourself
have the ability to shape your entire world.
speak intentionally.

the words you have with yourself are not insignificant—they are blueprints. every word you whisper in your mind builds walls or tears them down, opens doors or locks them shut. what you choose to tell yourself becomes the lens through which you see the world, the filter through which you measure your worth. if you call yourself unworthy long enough, the world will start to echo it back to you. if you remind yourself that you are capable, beautiful, resilient, the world will eventually rearrange itself to honor that truth. your inner dialogue is not background noise; it is the foundation of your becoming. speak with intention. speak with kindness. speak in ways that make your spirit want to rise instead of hide. let your words to yourself be the soft landing your heart can always trust, the daily reminder that you are not your mistakes, not your delays, not your doubts; you are the possibility of everything good still on its way. *your tongue is a compass. your language is a seed.* speak life, and watch your entire world bloom in response.

AUGUST 8TH

your mind is a garden.
water it with beautiful thoughts.

your mind is a garden. everything you think, everything you allow to linger, is a seed. some seeds will blossom into joy, peace, and clarity, others into doubt, fear, and resentment. the harvest of your life will always reflect what you've chosen to plant and what you've chosen to pull out. this is why your thoughts matter. the quiet conversations you have with yourself when no one else is listening are shaping you in ways you cannot yet see. the way you speak to your own heart will either nourish your spirit or drain it. you cannot expect to grow flowers from seeds of neglect. you cannot expect abundance from soil you've abandoned. so water your mind with beautiful thoughts. speak to yourself with tenderness. tell yourself you are capable, tell yourself you are worthy, tell yourself you are enough over and over again until your roots start to believe it. *the most important landscape you will ever tend is the one inside you.*

AUGUST 9TH

understand that anger is a valid response.
it is a powerful emotion,
it is a normal feeling.
how you channel it is where the real magic lies.
anger doesn't have to be destructive,
it doesn't have to be toxic;
it can be healing.

AUGUST 10TH

you deserve depth.

you feel unfulfilled because the connections you keep and the interactions you entertain don't fill you, you feel unsatisfied because the things you pour into don't reciprocate your energy in ways that speak to you, you feel empty because the people and situations you invite to your table don't feed your soul in ways you deserve. if you have to force it into existence more than it flows, then maybe it just isn't for you; if you have to abandon your intellect to be understood, then maybe they just aren't for you; if you have to sacrifice your authenticity to meet them at a surface level, then it isn't worth swimming for. *don't drown yourself in hollow energy when your intentions deserve depth.*

AUGUST 11TH

too many times you've left your self-worth unattended while trying to fulfill everyone else's needs, too many times you've neglected your happiness while trying to make everyone else comfortable, *too many times you've freely given out energy that you should be giving yourself.*

AUGUST 12TH

happiness is contagious, but it's also enviable. some will view your glow with bitterness; others will listen to your laughter with resentment, but this is why you must *protect your energy.* so that, regardless of what they do or don't do, they can never steal your peace.

AUGUST 13TH

if one day at a time is as fast as you can take it,
take each day as it comes
you are not required to live life all at once
you are not required to have everything figured out all at once
you are allowed to experience it all as delicately,
as patiently, and as slowly as you need

AUGUST 14TH

no one could ever complete you, but the right people have a way of amplifying your magic.

there's nothing more beautiful than having someone hold space for you while you're figuring out how to navigate through your roughest moments. there is nothing more necessary than connections that manage to breathe life into you regardless of how hard the world tries to suffocate you. there's nothing more fulfilling than being surrounded by energy that doesn't require you to be perfect but just requires you to be *you.*

AUGUST 15TH

there are some stories that will never belong to you no matter how hard you try to make a happy ending. some things can never be changed even if you have the best intentions.

there's nothing quite as dangerous to your mental well-being and nothing quite as damaging to your self-worth as consistently making excuses and exceptions for people who have shown you repeatedly that they aren't worth second chances or your accessibility. it can be pretty easy to get accustomed to mistreatment when it's coming from someone you care about or someone you love. it can be difficult to navigate through when you're in the process of unlearning people-pleasing tendencies or breaking toxic cycles, but it's so important to remember not to forget about you. *anything or anyone that takes you away from yourself isn't worth sacrificing your peace for,* and when you become aware of that imbalance, it's up to you to make adjustments that suit the kind of life and energy you wish to receive. may you find comfort in being true to yourself even if it means losing things or people that you thought were meant to stay.

AUGUST 16TH

you left the past behind for a reason.

sometimes it takes an unexpected person leaving for you to realize just how detrimental they were to your growth or the version of yourself that you're trying to become. sometimes it takes someone you weren't expecting to leave for you to realize just how damaging they were to your self-love or the life you're trying to build. when you *learn to look at people's exits as blessings,* you transform your entire outlook from what may seem like a low into something much warmer and more positive. what may not make sense in the moment will make sense eventually, but for now, allow their exit to unlock doors that you never knew needed to be opened.

AUGUST 17TH

don't attach guilt to your need for self-care.

don't let guilt stain the act of caring for yourself. self-care is not selfish; it is sacred. tending to yourself first is not neglecting others; it is preparing yourself to love them better, from a place of fullness. the ones who truly see you, the ones who truly value you, will never oppose your boundaries. they will understand why you sometimes have to step back, why you sometimes have to be quiet, why you sometimes need to choose solitude over company. they will know that your absence is not rejection; it is restoration. those who don't understand were never meant to drink from your well in the first place. water your own garden. rest without apology. heal without explanation. the love you give yourself becomes the love you're able to give the world.

AUGUST 18TH

there is nothing more beautiful than someone being intentional with you.

exchanges with substance feed into deeper awareness. open dialogue holds the key to unlocking closed hearts. honesty creates language that is fluent to the soul. sometimes we spend so many hours conversing for the sake of being social, exerting energy we don't have in the hopes of avoiding loneliness, indulging in what doesn't speak to us for shallow companionship; but true intimacy is built through purposeful action. committing time to listening so you can learn how to love better; sharing ideas, thoughts, and hopes that go beyond the physical; asking questions that stimulate the mind and soothe the nervous system; creating a safe space for their opinions and experiences so they can hopefully do the same for you. intimacy is not exclusive to romantic connections, nor is it immune to platonic ones. *be intentional about the energy you put into your relationships,* friendships, and partnerships so they can blossom freely as you grow along with them.

AUGUST 19TH

sometimes it's not about second chances after forgiveness
but moving forward with greater awareness.

know when to stop putting energy into things that you can't change, know when to stop putting time into what takes away from your peace, know when to stop committing effort into what pulls you away from yourself. the love you have for someone shouldn't be an excuse to stay in spaces that aren't conducive to your mental health, spaces that are detrimental to your growth, or spaces that poison the person you're trying to become. *love yourself enough to know when to leave bad love alone.*

AUGUST 20TH

where you are is exactly where you need to be to get to where you want to be.

learning to accept who you are currently and to be present with where you are is the cheat code to manifesting what you desire or what you deserve. sometimes we know deep down that we deserve more from our current circumstances or situations; sometimes we know deep down that we deserve to reap more from our effort and hard work, but *sometimes waiting on divine timing is more important than what we think we deserve.* it can be incredibly frustrating, having to wait for what we think we should be attracting or what we believe we should be receiving, but being grounded and finding gratitude for what you already have eases the tension and provides perspective to your plight.

AUGUST 21ST

your thoughts will make you a prisoner in your own mind if you're not careful.

nature isn't just a backdrop; it's a refuge. surrounding yourself with trees, sitting by water, or even just letting a gentle breeze touch your face is like stepping into a cleansing breath, washing away the tension and burdens that accumulate from the confines of the world. *spending time in nature offers a brief escape from stress,* honey for your rougher phases, a dose of much-needed perspective. it offers a humbling reminder that you are a part of something bigger, a participant in a grander story, an observer in the universe's great design. immerse yourself in the sights, sounds, and smells of the world. let the rhythm of leaves soothe your anxiety and the chirping of birds become your inner music. let the swiftness of the wind carry your worries and the sight of blooming flowers calm your nervous system.

AUGUST 22ND

some bridges must be burned so you have no choice
but to look forward even when you're tempted to look back.

sometimes we fall into the habit of normalizing people's mistreatment of us as a means of preserving the peace or maintaining a friendship or relationship that isn't conducive to who we are or who we are becoming, but *feel no guilt for putting a stop to what has cost you pieces of your mental health* or what doesn't sit well with your spirit anymore. feel no shame for creating new avenues by setting fire to older ones you've outgrown so you can find pathways that lead you back home.

AUGUST 23RD

the conditions don't need to be perfect for you to start.
you can start now, today,
exactly where you are,
without waiting for the weather to be in your favor.

AUGUST 24TH

release yourself from the pressure of having to be in flow at every single moment.

it's challenging to show up as your authentic self on certain days, difficult to embody your fullest identity in certain phases, hard to stay soft in some of your rougher moments, but you are still deserving of love through it all. it's easy to attach yourself to guilt when you're not showing up how you want to, easy to sink into impostor syndrome when you feel misaligned with who you're trying to be, easy to fall into traps of comparison when everyone else's garden looks greener than yours, but you are still deserving of grace through it all. *life won't always be in constant flow, and neither will you;* keep swimming until the waves find you again.

AUGUST 25TH

healing your standards will come with lots of silence
healing your standards will come with lots of solitude
healing your standards will come with lots of
misunderstanding and loneliness
but this is still healing

AUGUST 26TH

don't abandon who you are becoming to fit into boxes that make you more consumable.

you've worked too hard, in the shadows and in silence, to let anyone who doesn't know the amount of energy you've put into yourself tarnish the identity you are trying to maintain. *find the courage to accept and welcome in who you authentically are now,* even if it's misunderstood or makes anyone else uncomfortable.

AUGUST 27TH

their brokenness isn't yours to mend
their emptiness isn't your void to fill
their sadness isn't yours to cure
don't let a savior complex keep you stuck in cycles
that are meant for other people to break

AUGUST 28TH

holding everyone's worries and concerns will wear your spirit down over time.

every worry and every concern shared by others finds a place to rest within you. you hold them softly, weaving their fears into the fabric of your own thoughts, but there is only so much space within you, a limited capacity to carry the burdens of others before your own worries are crowded out. each worry you embrace from everyone else minimizes the space for your own dreams to flourish, for your own serenity to find a resting place, for your own peace to take root. it's a delicate balance to provide empathy and support without sacrificing your own well-being in the process. *offer compassion without shouldering the worries that rightfully belong to others.* your kindness is a gift, but never let it come at the expense of your peace.

AUGUST 29TH

honor the energy that remains from connections that have ended.

honor what once was, even if it no longer fits who you are. not every connection is meant to follow you into every chapter, not every connection is meant to stand by your side when you flip certain pages. *sometimes love ends not because it failed but because awareness shifted,* sometimes paths separate not because of anger but because healing demanded a different direction. when you outgrow certain bonds, it doesn't erase their meaning. it doesn't make the laughter less real or the lessons less sacred; it simply means you've stepped into a version of yourself that no longer aligns with the frequency they are choosing to live on. hold gratitude for what those connections gave you, and let them rest in peace without bitterness. awareness is not always shared at the same time, and that's okay. the healed version of you deserves to be surrounded by energies that match its depth, its softness, its clarity. release without resentment. honor without holding on. some chapters are meant to be closed so that your spirit can move freely into the next one.

AUGUST 30TH

in the right spaces, you won't have to shout to be heard
you won't have to shine a flashlight on your wounds to be seen
you won't have to change the language in your
soul's dictionary to be understood
you will be able to *come as you are* without having to alter your identity

AUGUST 31ST

being gentle in a world that hardens your spirit is a superpower.

a round of applause for you—for remaining soft through all the trials and tribulations you've had to endure, for remaining whole through all that has threatened to break you or steal your peace, for remaining full of love despite the lack of reciprocity you've received. so many things could've hardened your heart and poisoned your spirit, but you've managed to turn all those experiences into growth, all that pain and confusion into fuel for love, and become more you in the process. so, a round of applause for you—for still being here, for still holding warmth, for still choosing you. *you deserve celebration.*

solstice.

SEPTEMBER

soften my worries, and thicken
my faith. let intuition be the
compass that guides me
toward everything that is meant
for me, while giving me the
awareness to steer away from
any distractions. feed my spirit
with love, and fill my
dreams with direction.

SEPTEMBER 1ST

loving who you are now while working on who you want to be is the cheat code.

loving who you are now while working on who you want to be is the balance most people overlook. it is the secret, the quiet cheat code. too often we delay our love until we've arrived at some imagined destination, until we've perfected every flaw, until we've checked every box, but if you cannot love yourself in the middle, you will not know how to love yourself at the end. growth and self-acceptance are not enemies; they are companions. you can honor who you are in this moment and still move toward who you're becoming. *you can celebrate your progress while also tending to the places that require healing.* you can be both a work in progress and a masterpiece at the same time. the key is refusing to withhold love from yourself, because love is not a reward for completion; it's the fuel for transformation. the more you embrace who you are now, the easier it becomes to step into the person you're meant to be. love yourself as you are. build yourself as you go. that is the real shortcut.

SEPTEMBER 2ND

it's so important to learn when to let go
of what weighs you down more than it frees you.

there is so much freedom in letting go but moving accordingly. *forgiveness isn't always an automatic invitation for someone to return into your space,* it isn't always an indication that things can go back to how they once were, it isn't always a sign that the door leading to your heart is open again; sometimes it's just a simple intention to give yourself peace by choosing not to hold hands with pain or the people who caused you so much of it.

SEPTEMBER 3RD

the changes taking place in your life currently might be uncomfortable, the repositioning you are currently experiencing might be intimidating, the shifts you are currently trying to balance out might be frightening, but look at this as *a sign of the universe shuffling the deck in your favor for you to finally win.*

SEPTEMBER 4TH

no one owns your magic but you.

your magic was stitched into you long before you knew its name. it cannot be borrowed, it cannot be traded, it cannot be stolen. it is the fingerprint of your soul, the way you think, the way you love, the way you rise again and again when life tries to scatter you. many will try to mirror you, to echo your steps, to replicate your shine, but imitation is only surface. it will always fall short of the depth that lives within you. what is born from your heart cannot be duplicated by hands that were never shaped to carry it. your magic is not a costume that can be worn. it is not a skill that can be mastered by watching you closely enough. it is the sum of your scars and your victories, the rhythm of your breath, the voice of your inner world. it lives in the way you move through grief, in the way you choose joy despite uncertainty, in the way you find beauty in places others overlook. so protect it, not out of fear that it will be taken but out of reverence for how sacred it is. honor the fact that what flows through you is singular, unrepeatable, irreplaceable. trust that the right people will recognize it and celebrate it, and the wrong people will never be able to touch it. no one can outshine you at being you. no one can outdream you at being you. no one can rewrite what was written specifically for you. *your magic is yours alone.*

SEPTEMBER 5TH

some people will love who you used to be more than who you are now, but it is not your responsibility to reprise older versions of you to feed their ego.

in the ever-evolving landscape of your existence, remember that growth is your birthright. a journey marked by transformation and self-discovery. it's not your duty to remain tethered to who you used to be or to remain attached to an older life simply to feed the ego of anyone who cannot digest your evolution. you are not obligated to fit into molds that others have cast for you, nor are you required to shrink yourself into the confines of their expectations. let go of the need to conform to outdated versions of yourself. versions of you crafted to satisfy the comfort zones of others. versions of you designed to appease their deepest insecurities. your growth may challenge those who have not walked your divine path, people who have never felt the fire of your struggles or the liberation of your victories, but it is not your responsibility to make them comfortable with your revolution. their discomfort is not a reflection of your worth but only a display of their resistance to change, and that's not something you can fix by being who you used to be. *you owe no explanations for your metamorphosis and no apologies for your magic.*

SEPTEMBER 6TH

the friction you feel exists because what you're
trying to hold on to doesn't belong to you
the resistance you feel exists because what you're
searching for isn't looking for you
let alignment find you instead of trying to force
what you aren't ready for into existence

SEPTEMBER 7TH

you won't have the emotional capacity to show up for some people on some days. these are moments for reflection and reenergizing, not for guilt.

you were never meant to be available to every voice. every need. every demand. on some days, your well will feel dry, your light will feel dim, and your spirit will crave silence over conversation, stillness over showing up. these moments are not failures; they are checkpoints, invitations to pause and notice where your energy is leaking, where your heart has been overextended, where your body has been carrying more than it was built to hold. they are sacred pauses disguised as weakness. you begin to see which connections feed you and which ones drain you, you begin to understand the difference between obligation and genuine care, you begin to recognize that love without balance quickly becomes self-abandonment. when you give yourself permission to unplug, to retreat, to simply breathe without the weight of performance, your soul begins to gather its strength again. you are reminded that you cannot pour endlessly without being poured into, that you cannot always be the healer without remembering to heal yourself. you are allowed to step away. you are allowed to guard your energy. you are allowed to choose yourself first, and in doing so, you are not failing others; you are preserving the version of you that can return to them whole, patient, and overflowing with love again. even the sun sets to rise again. your pauses are not endings; they are a part of your rhythm. they are proof that rest is not abandonment—it is alignment.

SEPTEMBER 8TH

not everyone deserves parts of you.
not everyone can handle parts of you.
not everyone will be able to accept parts of you,
but *your discernment is what keeps your flame burning*
and lights the way toward the ones who do.

SEPTEMBER 9TH

and yes, love is conditional sometimes.
but sacrificing your peace, your values, or who you are
just because you love someone
isn't a reason to tolerate them.

real love would never ask you to abandon yourself. it would never ask you to silence your truth, to betray your values, or to shrink who you are just to make someone else comfortable. that is not love but tolerance disguised as devotion. love should never be a prison where you barter your peace for companionship, it should never be a bargain where your worth is traded away to keep someone close. if loving them means losing yourself, then what you're holding on to is not love but fear. *anyone who truly loves you will never place you in a position where you have to sacrifice your peace to keep them.* they will meet you at your wholeness, not demand that you cut pieces of yourself away to fit their mold. sometimes love has to be conditional, because unconditional love without boundaries becomes self-abandonment. you can care deeply for someone and still choose distance, you can wish someone well and still release them, you can honor what they meant to you without letting them dishonor what you mean to yourself. love them, but love yourself enough to walk away when that love begins to cost you the very essence of who you are.

SEPTEMBER 10TH

you will survive this just as you survived everything that came before, but you will come out of this a little wiser, a little more aware, and a little stronger.

you will survive this, just as you survived every storm that tried to break you before. you've made it through nights that felt endless, through losses that felt unbearable, through chapters you never thought you'd see the other side of, and yet, here you are. this is no different. but survival is not the only gift waiting for you on the other side of this. you will come out carrying more than just scars; you will come out carrying wisdom. you will understand yourself in ways you didn't before. you will see your strength in ways you had overlooked. you will know what peace feels like because you've wrestled with chaos. every challenge reshapes you, every heartbreak refines you, every obstacle adds another layer of resilience to your spirit, and while it may not feel like it now, one day you'll look back on this moment and recognize it as another stepping stone—another reminder that you are stronger, softer, deeper, and more aware than you were before it happened. you are not just surviving. you are becoming, and the version of you emerging on the other side of this will thank you for holding on.

SEPTEMBER 11TH

this is when the true
healing begins.

healing begins the moment you stop waiting for words that may never arrive. for many of us, the heart lingers at the door of accountability, hoping one day it will open and release the closure we crave, but some people will never apologize. not because you don't deserve it but because they are not ready to see the harm they caused or to meet themselves with honesty. so you wait, replaying the pain, holding yourself hostage to an admission that may never come, but freedom lives in acceptance and understanding that their silence is not your burden to carry, that you do not need their apology to validate your healing. true healing begins when you decide to give yourself the closure they could not, when you choose to release the grip you've had on their shortcomings and instead hold on to your own peace. the apology may never come, but the healing will, because healing has always been yours to claim, not theirs to hand over.

SEPTEMBER 12TH

sometimes you heal
and become a completely different person.
other times you heal
and become a stronger version of the person
you were always meant to be.

one of the biggest misconceptions we make when we're healing is thinking that, through our growth, we should become a completely different or new person, when what our process is really meant to do is help us to become a much fuller and more healed version of who we are already. maybe *it's not about completely disregarding or discarding who you used to be* but building upon all the hard work and energy you've put into yourself already so you can become more connected to your truth.

SEPTEMBER 13TH

being loved and being loved in the way you deserve
to be loved are two different things.
some people love you because they think it's the right thing to do.
others love you in ways that speak fluently to all your love languages.

SEPTEMBER 14TH

your light is uniquely yours; no one can ever take it from you.
plenty will be attracted to it, but few will be able to handle it.
some will be intimidated by it but will still
try to emulate its brightness.
but your light is uniquely yours.
no one can ever dim what belongs to you.

SEPTEMBER 15TH

sharing mutual interests may be a sign of genuine connection or relatability. it may show that there are a few things that you have in common, reveal synergy in the understandings you have about certain things in the world, but never confuse this with compatibility. *not everyone you get along with immediately is good for you in the long term.*

SEPTEMBER 16TH

how you choose yourself will determine how you unlock the doors to every other part of your life.

self-acceptance is the key. without it, every room you enter will feel foreign, every relationship will feel shaky, every opportunity will feel temporary. you will always second-guess your place, always question your worth, always wonder if you belong, but the moment you choose yourself, the moment you decide that who you are is enough, everything begins to shift. how you choose yourself becomes the foundation for how you experience the rest of your life. when you choose yourself, you stop begging for validation because you already know your value. when you choose yourself, you stop settling for half love because you already know what fullness feels like. when you choose yourself, you stop forcing your way into rooms that dim your light because you've built a home where your light can shine without restriction. every door that leads to peace, love, clarity, or purpose requires the same key, and that key is you. not the watered-down version of you, not the version that contorts itself for approval, but the version of you that stands whole, unedited, unapologetic. the way you choose yourself determines what doors unlock. if you choose yourself with hesitation, doors will open halfway, if you choose yourself with doubt, doors will creak and stall, but if you choose yourself with certainty, if you walk in your truth fully, the right doors will swing wide and welcome you. the life you want is already waiting for you, but it will recognize you only once you recognize yourself. hold the key, turn it firmly, and trust that every lock worth opening will respond to your authenticity.

SEPTEMBER 17TH

remember, having love for them doesn't mean
that they must have love for you in return.

if you're pouring from a selfless cup, what they do with it shouldn't be your main concern.

SEPTEMBER 18TH

if it isn't making sense right now, maybe it shouldn't.
maybe instead of trying to break the code,
you should *let things unfold naturally*
so it can all make sense when the time is right.

SEPTEMBER 19TH

you are still whole even when you don't feel like it
even with all the broken windows,
scratches on the walls, and holes in the doors,
you are still whole even when you don't feel like home.

SEPTEMBER 20TH

the path back to yourself will not be linear.

healing is not a straight road. it bends, it circles, it doubles back, it takes you through places you never expected to go. you may try to retrace old steps, but they will not feel the same. you may try to return to old versions of yourself, but you will not fit there anymore. the route you once knew is no longer the one that leads home, because you are not who you were before the heartbreak, before the lessons, before the realizations that cracked you open. you are softer now in some ways, sharper in others; you see more clearly, you feel more deeply, you carry a wisdom you didn't have before, so the path back to yourself must also change. it will guide you through unfamiliar terrain, ask you to release what you once clung to, and invite you to trust places that feel uncertain, but every twist and turn is teaching you something about your own becoming. don't rush to find the shortcuts, don't mourn the fact that the old road is gone. the journey is different now because *you* are different now.

SEPTEMBER 21ST

be patient with this masterpiece you're becoming. you'll go through many lows before you see the progress you're trying to make, experience confusion before your path starts to make sense again, feel isolated before you're surrounded by truth, but *it's all part of a bigger plan.*

SEPTEMBER 22ND

happiness will find you again,
your smile will find you again,
your laughter will find you again.
every flower has its season.

happiness will find you again, even if right now it feels like it has forgotten where you live. joy has a way of circling back, showing up at your doorstep when you least expect it, reminding you that life has not run out of light for you. your smile will return. not the practiced one you give to make others comfortable but the genuine one that rises from somewhere deep inside you, the one that feels like home. your laughter will return, too, not forced, not borrowed, but spilling out of you with ease, the kind of laughter that heals. pain convinces you that joy is gone forever, but pain is only a season, and every season changes. every flower has its moment to bloom, and every heart has its moment to blossom again. what feels barren now is simply preparation, what feels empty now is simply soil being readied for something beautiful, trust that *happiness has not abandoned you; it is just waiting for the right season to arrive.* your joy will return. your smile will return. your laughter will return. the flowers always come back, and so will you.

SEPTEMBER 23RD

you will never find value in the same spaces
that make you question your worth.

the rooms that silence your voice will never teach you how to speak louder, the hands that mishandle your heart will never show you how to love yourself better, the environments that thrive on shrinking you will never be the places where you finally learn how to expand. worth cannot be discovered where it is constantly denied. you cannot expect to feel whole in spaces that profit off your brokenness, you cannot expect to feel valued by people who benefit from you doubting yourself. so the work becomes walking away, not because you don't care, not because love isn't there, but because you finally understand that staying is the same as surrendering your spirit. your value doesn't live there, your peace doesn't live there, your becoming doesn't live there. the places that are meant for you will not confuse you about your worth; they will remind you of it, reflect it back to you, echo it until you finally believe it. *the people meant for you will not ask you to earn your space; they will celebrate the fact that you take up space at all.* never forget: the proof of your value is not in how hard you fight to convince others; it's in how easily your spirit can rest when you are in the right place.

SEPTEMBER 24TH

don't dissolve what makes you unique because it is too complex for them to understand, too intricate for them to comprehend. *live even louder* than you did before so you can drown out their opinions with your magic.

SEPTEMBER 25TH

check your list of priorities.
is your name at the very top,
or does it not appear on the list at all?

how far do the things that you are so willingly able to do for other people reach back to you? how much do you do for other people that you are willing to do for yourself? everything starts with you, and if you're not treating yourself with the same kind of energy and respect that you treat them with, then you are only falling short of the kind of love and expectations you should always have for yourself. *remember the importance of watering yourself before grabbing a cup for everyone else.*

SEPTEMBER 26TH

this life will not come with a map, it will not give you directions telling you where to go, it will not come with instructions advising you on what roads to take, it will not point you in the nearest vicinity of where you need to be. all you can really do is *take a leap* and *learn as you go.* sometimes this is the deepest form of courage.

SEPTEMBER 27TH

you can't be everything to everyone.

you will have to come to terms with the fact that you will disappoint some people along the way. this is not a reflection of your worth or your intentions but a natural part of choosing the lanes that are true to you. as you navigate your path, there will be moments when your choices don't align with the expectations of others, moments when your decisions go in the opposite direction of their intended destination, moments when your opinion ruffles the feathers of people expecting you to help them fly, but disappointment is inevitable; it is a testament to the authenticity of your journey. *you will never be able to live a life that honors your true self while constantly bending to please everyone else.* disappointing others is not an act of betrayal but a necessary step in honoring your own magic, and it is in these moments of truth that you reclaim your power, steering your life in a direction that feels right to you.

SEPTEMBER 28TH

your existence is a gift. choose who gets to unwrap it wisely.

your love, your time, your presence—none of it is ordinary. you've grown used to your own light, so you forget that others are blessed simply by being near it. *not everyone is worthy of unwrapping what you hold inside.* not everyone has the gentleness, the care, or the awareness to handle you properly. some people want only to tear through you carelessly, to take what shines and discard what they don't understand. so choose wisely. choose the ones who see the value before the unwrapping. choose the ones who slow down, who notice the details, who understand that you are not something to be consumed but something to be cherished. your existence is a rare offering. protect it, honor it, share it only with those who know how to hold you without breaking you, because you are not just a gift—you are the kind of gift that changes the life of whoever receives it.

SEPTEMBER 29TH

you are much more than the potential you possess
and the prospect for love that you carry.
you've got too much gold glistening in your
soul to be kept as a reserve lover,
a backup friend, or a connection on standby.
know your worth beyond what they choose to see in you.

SEPTEMBER 30TH

the ocean always changes its rhythm, and you are no different.
the waves may be crashing now, but you will find your flow again.

as you grow, much will transform and much will change, things will go and things will stay, but how you embrace your shifts is what will ultimately bring you more peace or keep you stuck in chaos. *take anything that misaligns as a sign,* look at anything that flows as a message. everything that happens in your life and everything that doesn't isn't coincidental. open your arms to what comes your way, and don't force what resists; *learn and grow through the different waves that come and go.*

OCTOBER

clothe me in happiness.
allow me to shift attention from
what i haven't found so i can
appreciate what i already have.
let every breath i take be a
celebration of how much i've
withstood and be confirmation of
how much beauty is still to come.
rejuvenate my ambitions.

OCTOBER 1ST

the more you excuse their mistreatment of you,
the harder it becomes to set boundaries.

occasionally, you'll be met where people last knew you or where they last remember your boundaries being, and *sometimes it's necessary to reintroduce yourself with fresh sentiments that are in line with who you are becoming* to preserve connections, to create deeper ones, or to maintain the ones you should be having with yourself. establishing or reestablishing these boundaries is how you create a stronger sense of self and reduce the friction that comes with anyone pushing you away from your growth or shaking loose pieces of your newfound identity. may the connections you build and the ones you maintain be rooted in healthy boundaries, and may you find the courage to step up for yourself if the energy ever changes.

OCTOBER 2ND

reject the advances of self-doubt and put trust in who you are.

it will come softly at first, whispering that you are not enough, that you are not ready, that you do not have what it takes. if you listen too long, it will start to sound familiar, it will start to sound convincing, it will start to sound like truth, but self-doubt is far from that—it is fear dressed as protection. trust in who you are. trust the path that has shaped you, the storms you have survived, the lessons you have carried. none of it was by accident. none of it was wasted. there is a strength inside you that doubt can never erase, wisdom that hesitation can never silence. *belief in yourself is one of the highest frequencies you can live on.* it changes the way you move, the way you attract, the way you open doors. when you choose belief over doubt, you step into alignment with everything that was meant for you, and in that space, nothing can keep you small.

OCTOBER 3RD

don't take your moments of clarity for granted.
you are understanding and realizing things
in this precise moment
for a *deeper and divine reason.*
document it, understand it, absorb it.

OCTOBER 4TH

"happily ever after" shouldn't be the end goal of every relationship or connection.

in some of the pages of our lives, we often search for a fairy-tale ending in which love blooms forever in perpetual bliss. but with time we learn that *happily ever after isn't a destination that can be reached in every connection.* true connection transcends the confines of good endings; it's about growth, about perspective, about learning from each other and becoming better versions of yourself through the mirrors of those we hold close. cherish every connection that shapes you. even if it didn't last forever, it still had something profound to teach you.

OCTOBER 5TH

show up in this lifetime
imperfectly
with no filter
with no disguise.
show up exactly as you are,
flawed but more than enough.

there is still much more to come for you regardless of where you feel like you are in your journey, regardless of how you may feel about yourself or the ideas you currently hold, regardless of how much you have achieved and what you haven't managed to live up to so far. *your potential is limitless, and everything else is limited by your mind and how you think of yourself;* you're allowed to exist as both the art and the artist of your life. may you never lose the desire to re-create yourself endlessly, and may the enthusiasm to continue blooming into whoever or whatever you need to be never end.

OCTOBER 6TH

one uncomfortable step at a time will still get you to where you need to be.

progress does not always look graceful. sometimes it looks like stumbling forward, sometimes it feels like crawling, sometimes it feels like dragging yourself through a season you would rather skip. but every small, awkward step is proof that you are still moving. the journey will not always be pretty. healing will not always be soft. growth will not always look inspiring. some days it will feel slow, some days it will feel ugly, some days it will feel like you are going nowhere at all. but the truth is, forward is forward, no matter the pace, no matter the posture. do not measure your growth by how polished it looks from the outside. measure it by the fact that you keep choosing to continue and by the courage required to take the next step even when the ground feels unsteady. *beauty isn't found just in the destination; it is found in the resilience you build along the way.* you may not see it yet, but every uncomfortable step is shaping you; one day you'll look back and realize that the slow and messy path still brought you to exactly where you were meant to be.

OCTOBER 7TH

your healing will require a lot of accountability.

while you're healing, it can be pretty easy to fall into the habit of taking your pain personally and lose perspective of how you may have contributed to your own wounds. *your healing requires complete honesty and transparency from your end* regardless of the part other people may have played in your aching. it requires a deep dive of introspection so you can see how to navigate in the future, it requires an open mind and heart to see what you should and shouldn't accept going forward, it requires full acceptance of everything you may have done when you were operating out of survival, fear, or lack of understanding. may you find the courage to look at yourself in the mirror with softness instead of judgment so you can open up more pathways that lead you back to yourself.

OCTOBER 8TH

finding fault in everything stops you
from seeing the light that exists.

life was never designed to meet every expectation you hold for it. sometimes the cracks will show, sometimes the edges won't line up, sometimes the picture won't match the one you carried in your mind, and that's okay. it doesn't always have to be ideal. waiting for flawless conditions will only keep you waiting. joy can be found in imperfect places, peace can be found in unfinished chapters, beauty can be found in things that don't match the script you imagined. if you are always searching for what is missing, always finding fault, you'll miss the light that was already shining. you'll miss the laughter hidden in the chaos, the love wrapped inside the flaws, the lessons tucked between the broken pieces. *perfection is not the goal—presence is.* allowing yourself to see the good that exists alongside the bad. choosing to notice the light, even when shadows are near. there is always something worth holding on to, always something worth being grateful for, always some glimmer that reminds you: imperfection doesn't make you unworthy.

OCTOBER 9TH

don't let fear of the unknown block you from receiving unexpected blessings.

the smallest of steps still matter. growth rarely lives in the spaces you've memorized, in the routines you've mastered, in the walls you've built for safety. it waits for you just beyond the familiar, in the places that stretch you, in the moments that ask more of you than you thought you could give. feel the energy, even if it is unfamiliar. discomfort is not danger; it is often a sign that you are entering new territory, that you are brushing against the edges of possibility. lean into that feeling, breathe into it, let it remind you that you are alive and becoming. don't let fear of the unknown block you from receiving what is already trying to find you. the blessings you are praying for may not look how you expect, and they may not arrive where you feel safest. sometimes they live in the risks you're afraid to take, in the conversations you hesitate to start, in the doors you're unsure about opening. *life expands when you do.* the more you trust yourself to move into the unfamiliar, the more you will discover how much has been waiting for you all along.

OCTOBER 10TH

everything you want is already on the way to you
everything you want is already being prepared for you
everything you want is already in alignment with you
everything you want is already yours
claim it

OCTOBER 11TH

focus on you, and let the distractions evaporate into the background.

fill your own cup first so you can pour back into connections that pour into you. sometimes the best way to help the people around you is by helping yourself first, even if that looks somewhat confusing on the outside, even if it doesn't make sense to everyone else, even if it feels briefly isolating or lonely, even if it seems selfish or misguided. *sometimes working on the connection you have with yourself is how you make the relationships in the rest of your life work.*

OCTOBER 12TH

what you've outgrown has nothing new to teach you.

returning back to expired energy won't make something new grow in its place, revisiting what isn't changing won't miraculously turn the odds in your favor, reintroducing yourself to older timelines won't erase written narratives; *accept what is for what it is.* some connections end up simply being lessons to help us remember who we are, reminders to never settle for lukewarm energy, and the signs that we need to lead us back into our own arms. embrace the temporary nature of certain connections, the abrupt or sudden endings of others, and the transient energy of relationships that you thought would last forever but ended up being a brief chapter in your story. all these connections played a pivotal role in who you are and who you are becoming. find gratitude for what they've shown you without trying to resurrect them, find acceptance for what they've become without trying to reopen old doors. *don't resist the waves; swim in them instead.*

OCTOBER 13TH

your new beginning will feel uneasy at first
it will feel rough in pockets
outgrowing who you used to be to step into who you want to be
will feel uncomfortable before it feels warm

OCTOBER 14TH

a whole world exists within you.
be selfish with whom you allow to travel within your borders.

your energy is precious; you're a rare and irreplaceable jewel. *being selective about whom you allow to hold you is not selfish but a recognition of your intrinsic value.* it's about understanding that not everyone who knocks on the door of your life deserves to step inside, it's about realizing that not everyone who gazes in your direction deserves your attention, it's about taking your self-preservation as seriously as you take yourself. your world is a garden, and you have every right to be discerning about where you plant your seeds; give your time to those who water your roots and those who help you grow and flourish. surround yourself with souls who match your frequency, those who understand that your presence is a privilege and not a right. every second wasted on the wrong people is time stolen from the right ones, so choose wisely. be with those who uplift you, those who see the light in you and reflect it back; be with those who bring peace to your chaos, those who bring serenity to your spirit. you are not obligated to entertain everyone who seeks your company. being selfish about whom you allow into your life is how you keep your worth intact and protect your energy from anyone with unclear intentions.

OCTOBER 15TH

like the moon
every version of you that you are
and every version of you that you've been
is *full of light*
and deserving of love
in all your phases

OCTOBER 16TH

trust your timeline.
you are perfectly placed for your awakening.

there's so much more to come from you, so much potential waiting for you to tap into, so much sweetness on the cusp of being found, and that isn't even the tip of the iceberg. there will never be a finality to who you are, a completion in the levels you can reach, a curtain call to who you are becoming, but this is the beauty in it all. *you can become whoever you want to become whenever you want, and the power exists solely in your hands,* the blueprint to your liberation belongs firmly in your grasp, the catalyst to better versions of yourself are limited only by your imagination and perceptions. it's never too early and never too late to be who you want to be; *you're right on time.*

OCTOBER 17TH

release yourself from the need to prove yourself, from the heaviness that comes with wanting to show people your worth, from the attachment that comes with trying to change people's opinions of you. *the only validation you need is your own.* everything else is just a distraction.

OCTOBER 18TH

the breakthrough you've been waiting for is just around the corner.

it can be so rough remaining patient while you're healing, so difficult to break out of conditioning while crossing your fingers for a development, so hard to wait for what you believe you deserve when you've been waiting for so long already. it's easy to lose sight of what's important in the midst of our low phases and so easy to get wrapped up in misery because it's taking time to obtain what we want to achieve, to get to where we want to be, or to embody how we truly want to feel. but everything you're experiencing is not without reason, everything you're battling is not without gain, everything you're feeling is not without its lessons. *you are exactly where you need to be even when it feels like you aren't.*

OCTOBER 19TH

you will meet three types of people in this lifetime—
those who teach you love,
those who teach you how to love yourself,
and, if you're lucky,
those who teach you both.

OCTOBER 20TH

sometimes you'll get what you want,
but the way you attract it will look entirely different
from what you expected.

life has a way of honoring your prayers while also reminding you that your vision is limited. you may ask for strength and receive struggle to build it. you may ask for love and find it in places you never thought to look. you may ask for clarity and be led through confusion that forces you to see more clearly. the way you attract what is meant for you will often look different than you expected. it won't always arrive on the timeline you set, and it won't always follow the path you planned, but that doesn't make it any less yours. sometimes the detours are the delivery. sometimes the delays are the alignment. sometimes the unfamiliar path is the only one that could bring you the gift in its truest form. so release the grip on how you think it should unfold. let go of the picture you painted in your head. trust that even if the process looks different, the outcome will carry what you truly need. life listens; the universe responds. *what is yours will find you, just not always in the way you thought it would.*

OCTOBER 21ST

deep-rooted connections
see you when you aren't seeing yourself.
they are your eyes in the world when self-doubt
has left you blinded.

genuine connections and friendships will never take it personally if you're in phases where you can't show up as your full self in the midst of your healing or your low points. they won't attach any projections to your distance or view your unavailability as malicious, they won't create false narratives because your story has landed on a difficult chapter. *they'll simply accept that you need yourself more than anyone else in that moment* and afford you as much time and patience as you need while you figure out what lesson life is trying to teach you. there's nothing more comforting than knowing that you are still loved and cared for regardless of what you're going through, there's nothing more assuring than knowing that you don't have to put on an act or a facade to maintain relationships with people you care about, there's nothing more beautiful than knowing that who you are and what connections you keep are not indications of your value or self-worth. *there's nothing more fulfilling than selfless connections that never lose sight of the real you.*

OCTOBER 22ND

you're wondering if you deserve better because deep down you know that you do.

OCTOBER 23RD

i am soaked in love and manifesting the kind of life i want to live.
i am divinely protected, and my intentions are dripping with abundance.

pushing through regardless of everything that's threatening your peace, persevering regardless of every obstacle that is standing in your way, prioritizing yourself regardless of how hard it is on some days—you deserve to be celebrated and much more. be proud of yourself; it takes a lot of strength and courage to be yourself, but *you're doing the best you can under the circumstances,* and all that deserves applause, even if it's just you clapping for yourself.

OCTOBER 24TH

understand that your stagnant stages that seem impassable are only temporary; the mental roadblocks that you struggle to maneuver past are momentary. *inspiration comes in waves, and it will find you again* once you learn how to swim in this phase.

OCTOBER 25TH

every connection you keep is a mirror.
they are each a reflection of how much love you have for yourself
or how much healing you still have to do.

OCTOBER 26TH

it is a privilege to get to know yourself all over again, to leave behind who you used to be and meet who you want to be, to reintroduce yourself to the world as a new embodiment of who you knew you always were, to *reacquaint yourself with your magic.*

OCTOBER 27TH

energy has been your first language since birth.
heartache may have made you a little rusty with your comprehension,
but you can never forget a dialect in which you're fluent.

words and actions mean only so much if the energy behind them and the feelings they leave you with aren't taken into consideration. your gut instinct is one of your most powerful tools, and sometimes your nervous system is simply asking you to exercise discernment when something doesn't sit right with your spirit after your interactions with certain people. don't leave your intuition on read whenever it is trying to get your attention, don't ignore your body when it goes into high alert; people can be dishonest, actions can be deceiving, but *energy never lies.*

OCTOBER 28TH

your future self is thanking you for all the hard work and energy you're putting into your endeavors right now, happy that you stayed on course and didn't choose to give up, proud that you kept your head up after encountering things that could've sunk you, celebrating that you didn't let any obstacles discourage you from moving forward. don't let up now; *keep going.*

OCTOBER 29TH

when you begin to live in your truth, your intentions evict everything that isn't meant for you, your energy becomes a placeholder for honesty, and your spirit rejects anything that isn't authentic. the locks to your heart become accessible only to those living in their truth, too.

OCTOBER 30TH

the things you put on a pedestal become the things that consume you. choose wisely.

what you glorify will eventually shape the way you see yourself, the way you measure your worth, the way you navigate your days. if you place your value in the hands of others, you will always be chasing their approval. if you worship what you lack, you will always live in a state of scarcity. if you exalt fear, you will always move from a place of limitation. choose wisely. not everything deserves your reverence, not everything deserves your loyalty. be mindful of what you bow to, be mindful of what you allow to own your attention, energy, and devotion, because *whatever you elevate above yourself will eventually become the thing that defines you.* remember, you were never meant to be consumed; you were meant to be free. build your pedestals carefully, and only place what helps you rise on them.

OCTOBER 31ST

be grateful for everything and every person who revealed their true intentions, even if it wasn't what you wanted. now you can move forward with no illusions of who's with you and who isn't.

be grateful for everything and every person who revealed their true intentions, even if it hurt, even if it wasn't what you wanted to see. *truth is always a gift, even when it arrives in disappointment.* clarity is always a blessing, even when it comes wrapped in loss. every mask that slips, every single word that exposes, and every action that reveals what was hidden are not betrayals of your path but confirmations. now you know who is really with you and who was only passing through. now you can stop pouring into hands that could never hold you. now you can stop chasing connections that were never rooted in truth. what you gained is freedom, the freedom to no longer live under illusion, the freedom to walk lighter because you're no longer carrying what was false. it may sting at first, but it clears the way for the right people, the right energy, and the right love to find you.

NOVEMBER

wrap silk around my doubts.
add softness to the opinion i have
of myself, and refill my cup with
patience every time i lose sight
of who i am. allow me to stop
holding hands with fear
so i may attract what is meant
to find me. evict uncertainty
so i may welcome in peace.

NOVEMBER 1ST

keep watering the reality you want to manifest
pour love on to the belief that what you want is already yours
put effort into the seeds you've already planted
and wait while something blooms from your intentions

NOVEMBER 2ND

the safest connections will never ask you to embody
a version of yourself that you've outgrown.
they'll never ask you to compromise your
identity to solidify their own.
the only thing they'll require from you is that you come
authentically as you are, regardless of how that looks.

NOVEMBER 3RD

as long as i remember the importance of watering myself,
i will always grow wherever i am planted.

when you discover and hold on to self-love and self-respect, you discover the resilience to blossom even in the most unexpected of circumstances, you find the stubbornness to grow even in the most unlikely of environments, you find the perseverance to bloom even in the most improbable of situations. like a delicate seed entrusted to fertile soil, *your growth begins with the soft care you put into yourself,* and as long as you prioritize your well-being by constantly watering yourself and your needs, you will always thrive wherever life plants you.

NOVEMBER 4TH

you are not required to be who people want you to be.

people's expectations of who they expect you to be can add unnecessary baggage to all the weight you may be carrying already. we absorb, normalize, and carry so much energy that doesn't belong to us because of trauma, responsibility, shame, and love, but rarely do we put our own feelings on a pedestal as a marker for where our standards should be. *anyone's projections, ideas, opinions, or perceptions aren't yours to keep,* and you don't have to feel guilty for dropping what continues to weigh you down.

NOVEMBER 5TH

some new doors will require you
to leave old versions of who you used to be
in order to unlock them.

some new doors will not open for the person you used to be. they require more of you, more honesty, more courage, more willingness to shed the layers that no longer serve you. *the keys that fit your old life will not unlock the places you're being called to step into now.* to move forward, you have to release the versions of yourself that were built for survival, the habits that once protected you but now only keep you small, the patterns that once felt safe but now keep you stuck. it is not a betrayal of who you were; it is an honoring of who you are becoming. growth often asks for a trade. it asks you to let go of comfort in exchange for possibility, to let go of familiarity in exchange for freedom, to let go of outdated identities in exchange for alignment. the doors ahead of you are sacred. they are not meant to be forced open by old keys. they are waiting for the version of you that trusts, the version of you that believes, the version of you that knows they are worthy of walking through. every step forward is not just about reaching new places; it's about becoming the person who belongs in those places.

NOVEMBER 6TH

if it was done out of love, then it was never a waste
if it was done out of love, then it was never a mistake
if it was done out of love, then it was never misplaced

NOVEMBER 7TH

find no shame in the moments
when you need your own energy
more than anyone else's.

masking your pain becomes a habit when you normalize being performative over being honest. sweeping your trauma under the rug won't speed up your healing or make the wound magically disappear. surrounding yourself with distractions won't provide you with permanent relief or lasting stability. *sometimes what you really need is you.* not anyone else's opinion, unsolicited advice, or energy, just time with yourself to unpack and understand why you're hurting while finding different routes to peace in your own company.

NOVEMBER 8TH

good spiritual hygiene
will require you to clean out old, expired energy
that has overstayed its welcome
so you can usher in energy more in line with who you're trying to be.

sometimes putting an end to toxic habits and people-pleasing tendencies means letting go of all the things that kept you in cycles that made you unrecognizable or unfamiliar to yourself. sometimes looking closely at your wounds and acknowledging how you played a part in your pain or heaviness is how you give yourself more chances to breathe in air that is more accommodating of who you are and who you are becoming. sometimes being honest about how you can do better and form healthier pathways is how you tap into that deeper awareness of what you deserve and what you shouldn't hold on to anymore.

NOVEMBER 9TH

your magic is only as potent as the people you surround yourself with.

nothing is quite as fulfilling as a romantic or platonic connection that adds more to your individuality without taking pieces away from what makes you, you. many situations inadvertently and subconsciously force you to walk away from yourself as a means of adding value to the energy that exists within a connection, but *the most powerful unions ask you to come as you are while encouraging you to grow into whoever you want or need to be.* appreciate those who see you for you and not who they desire for you to be; the connections that facilitate freedom for you to unapologetically be yourself will always fill your lungs with air.

NOVEMBER 10TH

be prepared to be misinterpreted
be prepared to be judged
be prepared for your entire being to be misunderstood
when you start walking down your authentic path

NOVEMBER 11TH

every chapter that closes is giving
you a chance to start a new story.

endings are not punishments—they are pivots. they arrive to shift your direction, to free your hands from what you were never meant to carry forever. trust the silence after the goodbye, trust the space that opens when something leaves, trust every single thing that ceases. what stops moving was not meant to sustain you any longer. what fades away was not meant to light your path forever. sometimes the closing of a door is the loudest form of protection. sometimes what feels like loss is really life's way of clearing space for something brighter. every chapter that closes is not just taking something from you; it is giving something to you. it is giving you clarity, it is giving you freedom, it is giving you the opportunity to write again, to create again, to dream again without the weight of what no longer belongs. new stories cannot begin if you are still clinging to the old pages. let them close. let them rest. trust that what comes next will honor the growth you've gained, the wisdom you've earned, and the person you've now become. *endings are not the end of you;* they are the beginning of new chapters in which you are stronger, softer, and more ready than you were before.

NOVEMBER 12TH

some connections will require you to reestablish your boundaries so you can be met where your healed standards are. they will require you to respect where you are currently instead of holding yourself to older expectations of who you used to be.

NOVEMBER 13TH

the more time you spend feeding one-sided connections,
the more you starve the connection you should be having with yourself.

when it's coming from a genuine and selfless space, it won't require you to walk away from yourself to see yourself clearly. it won't require you to abandon your self-worth, suppress your self-esteem, or neglect the things that you love about yourself to feed it. it won't require that you change your composition, tarnish your internal makeup, or carve a new identity for you to survive. instead, it will consistently encourage you to find routes that lead you back home to yourself, it will amplify the beautiful pieces that exist within you already instead of taking them away or destroying them, it will simply hold a mirror up with no judgment so you always recognize who you are and never lose sight of your unique journey. *you deserve love that wants to see you grow as you are, from where you are, and where you're intending to go.*

NOVEMBER 14TH

you can't love anyone out of their misery
you can't lead them into finding healing they
are unwilling to find for themselves
you can't force them to see their worth through your eyes
you can only be as present as you can for them
while letting them learn their lessons

NOVEMBER 15TH

you are allowed to change your mind on
what you were sure about before
you are allowed to outgrow old mindsets and ways of thinking
you are allowed to evolve without attaching shame
to your newfound levels of consciousness

NOVEMBER 16TH

everything will arrive when you are ready
at the right time
in the right moment
everything will arrive when you least expect it
have patience

NOVEMBER 17TH

the fullness of who you are will only be understood by those who have spent time trying to understand their own depths.

depth recognizes depth. only those who have taken the time to sit with their own shadows and have listened to the echoes of their own soul will have the patience and awareness to hold all of you. surface-level hearts will only skim the top of your waters. they will call you complicated, they will call you distant, they will call you "hard to love" because they cannot see beyond their own reflection. it is not your job to make yourself shallow just so they can understand you. the ones who have dived into their own depths, their own heartbreak, their own healing, their own transformation, will know how to meet you in yours. they will not flinch at your storms, they will not run from your intensity, they will not be startled by your silence; they will recognize you because they have already recognized themselves. protect your energy. honor your layers. do not dilute your fullness for those unwilling to explore their own. *you are not here to be easy to understand; you are here to be real.* the right souls will not only understand that—they will celebrate it.

NOVEMBER 18TH

you can dilute yourself and you'll still be too much for some people
water yourself down and still taste too strong
filter yourself and still be too intense
this is why you must be for *you* first
so that whether they accept who you are or don't
you still remain *enough for yourself*

NOVEMBER 19TH

never let who you didn't become dampen the fabric of who you are trying to be.

the new versions of you that you're stepping into will require fewer apology letters and more acceptance for your authentic self. as parts of who you used to be expire, so will the programming and the comfortability that came with those identities. *the things you lose and the skin you shed while inching closer to the fullest version of you are only making space for what's meant to stay.* detach yourself from external opinions, and quiet down your insecurities; allow your evolution to be as beautiful and as imperfect as you need it to be.

NOVEMBER 20TH

sit alone with your thoughts, spend time with your wounds,
take intentional time in solitude
so you can understand what baggage or blessings you're bringing
to the table in all your connections and interactions

NOVEMBER 21ST

know when to stop putting energy into things you can't change
know when to stop putting time into things
that take away from your peace
know when to stop committing effort to things
that pull you away from yourself

NOVEMBER 22ND

there is power in recognizing
cycles before you fall into them again.
there is magic in making
a conscious effort not to act on the familiar.

there is so much power in your shifts of awareness and the things you are able to identify before they happen, there is so much magic in tapping into a deeper understanding with yourself and realizing what takes you away from you. sometimes our older experiences make it difficult to see the full picture in front of us amid mental fog, and sometimes our past makes us unfamiliar to even ourselves, but as soon as you start to recognize the patterns and repeated habits, take it as a beautiful sign, take it as a good omen, take it as a key to higher consciousness; *it will take consistent practice to break certain cycles that you're stuck in, but the biggest step comes when you become aware of all the things that have been holding you back.*

NOVEMBER 23RD

what's happened has happened
what's to come will come
swim in the present for a while
enjoy the water
the waves have something to teach you

NOVEMBER 24TH

sometimes it will take more than just enforcing or communicating boundaries for people to truly understand how you want to be loved or treated.

eventually, it gets to a point where you have to ask yourself if your boundaries aren't clear enough or if it's a case of you simply inviting energy you don't want because you're consistently choosing to engage with what you've outgrown or tolerating what isn't conducive to you anymore. sometimes we get so lost in people-pleasing that we focus on how our boundaries are affecting other people while completely ignoring how a lack of boundaries is affecting us. if your feelings and concerns keep getting tossed to the wayside even after you've made how you feel as clear as you possibly can, feel no guilt in choosing the vibrationally higher path, feel no shame for heading in a direction where you are seen without having to overexplain your existence and the ways in which your feelings should be respected and honored. if it means having to keep some of you to you, or if it requires keeping your energy to yourself to maintain your peace, then so be it. *love from a distance is still love.*

NOVEMBER 25TH

you may not be where you want to be in this exact moment, but that doesn't mean you'll never get to where you want to be. be soft with yourself as you get there, take your time with everything that you are now; everything that you're experiencing behind the curtains and in the dark will bear fruit eventually.

NOVEMBER 26TH

worry not about what they have to say.
their opinions will fade,
but what you think of yourself will always remain.

people will always have something to add, some opinion to give, some version of you they'll try to write without ever knowing the whole story. their words may echo loudly for a moment, but echoes fade; the voices that once felt so heavy will grow faint with time. today's criticism will be tomorrow's silence. the same mouths that doubted you will eventually move on to something else, and you'll realize their judgment was never as permanent as it felt, but what you think of yourself will always remain. the way you speak to your reflection, the way you carry your heart, the way you stand in your own truth—this is what endures. your inner voice has more power than all the outside noise combined, so protect it. nurture it. let it be kind, let it be encouraging, let it be the loudest voice in the room. long after everyone else has gone quiet, you will still be left with yourself, and *what you think of yourself will shape everything that comes next.*

NOVEMBER 27TH

the glow can't be dimmed if the source is from within.

it's so important to constantly check in with yourself to make sure you're good, constantly ask yourself important questions to make sure you're in alignment with your goals, constantly refill your own cup when you've been pouring consistently into the people around you. it's never too late to start prioritizing yourself now if you weren't doing so before, to start catering to yourself now if you've been feeding everyone else's needs, to start remembering the unique placement you have in your own life. *it's never too late to start choosing you.*

NOVEMBER 28TH

if it goes wrong, you'll have lessons to learn.
if it goes to plan, it'll be exactly what you wanted.
each scenario is a win-win.
shift your perspective.

NOVEMBER 29TH

the beautiful thing about being your own muse is that you never have to be at the mercy of anyone's gaze to feel validated, you never have to rely on external energy to feel as if you are worthy of celebration. *you continue being art regardless of whether they see you or not.*

NOVEMBER 30TH

it's not rejection if it leads you back into your own arms.

rejection isn't always a closed door, a missed opportunity, or a chance gone by. sometimes it's a gentle nudge back to a path you may have forgotten, a soft shove leading you to where love feels like oxygen, a subtle push in the right direction. disappointment may feel like a chilling wind, but it can also clear away the clutter, allowing you to rediscover the warmth and comfort of your own inherent value. acknowledge the sting of rejection, the confusion of it, the disappointment in it, but never let it define you. use it as a springboard for introspection, a chance to explore your own desires and what truly brings you joy. as unpleasant as rejection feels, it can be a powerful compass, *a divine misdirection*, guiding you back to the comforting embrace of self-love.

DECEMBER

close the chapters that don't
speak to my spirit, and open up
the pages that remind me of who
i am. give me the courage to release
myself from what i've outgrown so
i can fit into shoes suited for where
my journey is going. balm me in
patience, and soak my
bones in love.

DECEMBER 1ST

visibility means nothing if you're tainting your authenticity just to be seen.

you will never have to step out of character or embody something that you aren't to attract the things that you truly deserve. sometimes we get so lost in wanting a desirable outcome that we let impatience ruin the harvest we've been working so hard to cultivate. *let your seeds come to fruition naturally instead of trying to make things sprout prematurely.* when the time is right, your flowers will bloom.

DECEMBER 2ND

the intimacy of someone holding a safe space for your thoughts, creating intentional time for you to be heard without being judged, shining light in corners of your mind that you've dimmed so you can be seen clearly, giving you the freedom to be felt on a soul level.

it's the friendships, relationships, and bonds that go beyond the surface to make you feel seen, the ones that go the extra mile to make sure you feel appreciated, the ones that work on comprehending you and your energy so you feel understood, the intentional connections. there are truly not many things more intimate than someone being intentional with their love for you so you can find different ways to love yourself and return that love back in their direction. *the right intentions set the tone for the rest of the connection and help you maintain your magic throughout.*

DECEMBER 3RD

slow down
this journey is a long one.

i hope you take this as your sign to stop trying to rush what isn't making sense and to stop trying to force what isn't in your control. *knowing what you deserve can be a double-edged sword* because, on one hand, you know deep down that you're worthy of so much more, but, on the other hand, waiting for it can become frustrating when it's taking longer than expected to come to fruition. remember, there's gold to be discovered in everything you experience while waiting for what you want to finally manifest.

DECEMBER 4TH

small signs are still signs.
don't lose sight of the bigger picture.

the softest breeze can signal a change in season. the faintest star can still guide a traveler home. not every confirmation will roar into your life; some will arrive quietly, like a whisper you'll almost miss if you aren't paying attention. the bigger picture is built out of these small moments: a glance that reminds you you're not alone, a chance encounter that shifts your perspective, a door that closes and teaches you patience. each individual moment may not look monumental on its own, but together they are shaping the path beneath your feet. when you're on the road toward your goals, you will feel tempted to overlook the details because your eyes are fixed on the horizon, but the horizon is stitched together by the small signs that appear along the way. the progress that feels too minor to celebrate is still proof that you are moving forward, the lessons that hurt are still proof that you are being prepared. *don't dismiss the breadcrumbs just because you wanted a feast,* don't dismiss the flicker just because you wanted a bonfire. the universe rarely hands you the destination all at once; it gives you directions in fragments, one sign at a time. and on the day when you finally arrive, you will realize that every small sign, every subtle shift, every almost invisible step, was necessary; the bigger picture could not exist without them. the small signs are not distractions from the journey—they *are* the journey.

DECEMBER 5TH

you will never have to look outside of yourself to find completion
you will never have to look outside of who you are to find wholeness
you will never have to abandon who you are to find what's truly for you

DECEMBER 6TH

sometimes overcoming yourself is the battle that will help you manifest your desired reality.

one of the biggest roadblocks you'll encounter as you inch closer to who you want to be will always be yourself. *there's no heavier shadow you'll have to deal with than your own,* no lower feeling you'll have to deal with than your deepest regrets, no ideas you'll have to heal as much as the ones attached to your old mistakes; there will be nothing more conflicting than dealing with what you can't change or control from the past. many karmic and generational cycles are asking to be broken but are waiting for you to show up, they're waiting for you to acknowledge their monotony and repetitiveness, they're waiting for you to be more present in the now instead of holding on to what has passed or what has yet to happen, they're waiting for your awareness to finally arrive so you can confront truth. the things we refuse to learn only keep us more embedded in who we used to be and not who we could be, the things we refuse to learn limit our potential and block pathways to our healing and growth, *the things we refuse to learn are the cycles we remain stuck in until the lesson is understood.* hoping that you understand your assignment or what pulls you away from it, hoping that you find the strength to let go of older habits to make space for healthier ones, hoping that you break out of what feels safe only because it's familiar; may you find love for all the things you are still healing from, and may your wounds become beautiful lessons and not permanent scars.

DECEMBER 7TH

whatever leaves or whatever you lose is just confirmation that it was never for you to begin with.

the things you lose and everything that disappears during your moments of clarity or when you're being honest with yourself were never for you to begin with. *what is yours will always be attracted to your truest self,* and what can't handle it will fade or fall by the wayside. you should never have to change yourself, alter who you are at your core, or erase your identity and principles to keep anyone or anything in your life. prioritize your growth, happiness, and peace of mind by putting your true self in everything you do regardless of what others may feel or how the world may react to it; *emancipate yourself so the authentic you always remains.*

DECEMBER 8TH

dance your way through all the transitions.

life will shift, seasons will change, relationships will evolve, dreams will stretch into new shapes. *nothing stays still forever, and that is the rhythm you are meant to move with.* don't resist it. let the transitions become your choreography, let them teach your feet new steps, let them teach your heart new ways to move; flow with the melodies and harmony changes of the universe. the song will not always sound the same; some verses will be soft and tender, others will roar with intensity. sometimes the rhythm will feel too fast to keep up with, other times it will feel painfully slow, but every note belongs. every beat has its place. when you surrender to the music, you'll realize you were never meant to control it; you were meant to feel it, you were meant to let it guide you. do it all with love. let love be the way you steady yourself when the transitions feel overwhelming, let love be the anchor that holds you during the beat changes. love for yourself, love for the process, love for the unseen forces carrying you forward, because when love is at the center, every step, whether graceful or clumsy, becomes holy. life will keep changing its tune, but you are allowed to keep dancing.

DECEMBER 9TH

come back into your own life. you've been missing for a while. lost in everyone else's energy, trapped by external perception, focused on distractions instead of your divine path. come back into your own life so the love you've abandoned finally finds you at home within yourself.

DECEMBER 10TH

what's for you will find you.

you can do the work, you can plant the seeds, you can water the soil—but *you cannot control how or when the harvest shows up.* clinging too tightly to one image of how it should be only blinds you to the infinite ways it could unfold. what's for you will find you not because you chase it endlessly, not because you demand it to appear on your timeline, but because what belongs to your spirit cannot miss you. the doors meant for you will open, even if they take longer than expected. the love meant for you will arrive, even if it doesn't look like the picture you painted in your head. the opportunities meant for you will align, even if the road there looks unfamiliar. even if it looks a little different when it arrives, trust that it's still yours. sometimes the universe answers your prayers in ways you didn't recognize at first glance. sometimes the blessing wears a disguise. sometimes the gift comes wrapped in a challenge, in a delay, in a detour, but if you pay attention, you'll see it was always for you. release the grip, let go of the script, be open to the unfolding. what is truly yours will never need to be forced; it will always find its way home to you.

DECEMBER 11TH

the work you do in your inner world magnetizes everything you attract externally.

the truth is, *some of the voids you feel can be filled only by you.* more intentional solitude with yourself, more dates with your wounds to find out why they still hurt, more time dedicated to everything that contributes to your growth, more energy committed to your healing, more patience and softness with yourself throughout your whole process.

DECEMBER 12TH

to know you aren't perfect but to also know you are still everything—this is magic.

there will always be voices that say you must polish yourself before you are worthy, voices that say you must earn your value, voices that measure you against impossible standards, but real freedom begins when you no longer argue with those voices. when you let them speak, let them fade and return to your own truth with the realization that even with flaws, even with mistakes, even with unanswered questions, you are still whole. you are still light. you are still a miracle. magic is not about removing what is broken; it is about realizing that broken things still shine. it is about understanding that the cracks in your spirit let love seep in, let wisdom grow, let depth form where there once was only surface. you don't have to be perfect to be radiant. you don't have to be flawless to be unforgettable. you don't have to have it all figured out to be deserving of love. *the magic is not in trying to be everything; the magic is in realizing you already are.*

DECEMBER 13TH

forgiveness isn't always an automatic invitation for someone to return to your space, it isn't always an indication that things can go back to how they once were, it isn't always a sign that the door leading to your heart is open again; sometimes it's just *a simple intention to give yourself peace by choosing not to hold hands with pain or the people who caused it.*

DECEMBER 14TH

your best moments are still on their way to you.
trust the postponements,
the delays, the brief pauses.
trust that *the best moments of your life are yet to be lived.*

DECEMBER 15TH

nectar will be dripping from your intentions
after all the endurance you've shown.
you will soon taste the sweetness of your patience.

all the effort you made in silence, all the prayers you whispered in the dark, all the acts of faith that felt unseen, are never forgotten. the universe has a way of collecting every drop of sincerity, every ounce of consistency, and returning them to you in abundance. you will soon taste the sweetness of your patience. patience that once felt heavy, patience that once felt like emptiness, patience that stretched you in ways you didn't know you could endure. you held on when letting go would have been easier. you kept moving when standing still seemed safer. you chose to trust when doubt was louder, and now life is preparing to pour goodness into your hands—not as a reward you had to earn but as a reflection of the faithfulness you've shown. every delay was refining you. every pause was strengthening you. *every detour was teaching you that good things ripen slowly,* that blessings take time to bloom, that nectar needs seasons before it can flow. when the time comes, sweetness won't just fill your senses; it will heal the bitterness of the waiting.

DECEMBER 16TH

may the distance between searching for your purpose
and walking in your purpose shorten
as you pour more love into yourself
and find a better understanding of who you are.

DECEMBER 17TH

the best blessings are the ones you receive without having to change a single thing about yourself to get them, the ones you attract just by being.

there isn't a more beautiful version of yourself than the one that is able to show up with no apology letters attached to your essence. free from opinions, detached from the ideas people try to project, distanced from assumptions that don't belong to you, *fully immersed in your truth.* let the things that flow your way be a reflection of the honesty and love you maintain with yourself, and let the things that don't remain be confirmation that *your magic and energy isn't for everyone.*

DECEMBER 18TH

*i am in alignment with everything my heart desires,
and everything i desire is in alignment with me.*

alignment is never about running faster or pushing harder; it's about trusting that the right things are already moving toward you, the same way you're moving toward them. *when your heart is clear about what it desires, life begins to respond.* doors start to open, opportunities begin to appear, and people cross your path in ways you couldn't have orchestrated on your own, but it happens only when you let yourself believe you are worthy of receiving. so instead of forcing, soften. instead of controlling, trust. remind yourself that what you want is not outside of you; it is a reflection of you. if it lives in your heart, it's because it was designed to meet you. be patient with the timing. be open to the form in which it arrives. alignment is not about perfection; it's about being in step with the truth that what's meant for you cannot miss you. everything your heart desires is already in alignment with you, waiting for you to stand fully in alignment with yourself.

DECEMBER 19TH

find peace in knowing that the waters won't be chaotic for an entire day.
at some point the waves will find their calm, and so will you.

DECEMBER 20TH

do not suffocate your mind by thinking too far ahead
do not drown your heart by staying in the past
find breath in this current moment
in this present timeline
in the now

there is beauty in finding the balance between what you want and what you have already. where you are deserves to be appreciated as much as where you're going, who you are deserves to be loved as much as who you are becoming, what you have deserves to be valued as much as what you wish to attract. *may you find everything your heart desires without losing sight of everything that has brought you this far.*

DECEMBER 21ST

the life you are creating won't be suitable for everyone.
it won't have space for everyone.
it will be a reality with which only a select few will be compatible.

as you grow, as you heal, as you step into alignment with who you truly are, your life will begin to take on a shape that not every hand can hold, not every spirit can match, and not every presence can honor. it won't have space for just anyone. the version of you that is unfolding is too intentional to carry every voice, too sacred to host every energy, too valuable to be stretched thin by people who don't understand what it took to get here. you are building a life that reflects your truth, and truth naturally eliminates what is false. it will be a reality with which a select few will be compatible. the ones who recognize your growth without being intimidated by it. the ones who celebrate your boundaries instead of resenting them. the ones who can match your love with their own depth, your vision with their own courage, and your energy with their own authenticity. don't grieve the fact that not everyone can come with you; *expansion requires release.* the more you honor that truth, the more space you create for those who are truly aligned to find their way to you. the right people won't just fit into your new reality; they will help it flourish.

DECEMBER 22ND

you don't have to wait for everything to be perfect for you to be happy.
don't rob yourself of the magical moments and beautiful vibrations
that come your way because you're not where you want to
be or because you're not who you want to be yet.
welcome everything good that comes your way with open arms.

DECEMBER 23RD

some things are better left unsaid, some things are better left unaddressed, some things are better kept to yourself until the time feels right. part of protecting your essence involves *discerning where you spill your thoughts and where you commit your energy so your magic can remain potent.*

DECEMBER 24TH

it's perfectly normal for you to feel exhausted after spending so long dedicating your time and energy to everyone else and what they have going on in their life, it's perfectly normal for you to get tired of neglecting yourself to tend to everyone else's battles. but sometimes all that is just your body trying to convey an important message to you, a message boldly declaring: *it's time to come home.*

DECEMBER 25TH

your existence is the greatest gift.
you being you is a blessing.

DECEMBER 26TH

you won't always feel seen,
you won't always feel accepted,
you won't always feel validated,
you won't always feel appreciated,
but the real power is in finding those feelings in yourself.
pay less attention to the external wins
so you can see the value in everything
happening for you internally.

DECEMBER 27TH

knowing yourself is a form of protection, too.

when you know who you are, you stop letting the world convince you otherwise. you stop shrinking to fit into spaces that were never designed for your spirit. you stop mistaking temporary opinions for permanent truths. self-knowledge is a shield. it guards you against manipulation, against comparison, against the temptation to abandon yourself just to be accepted. when you know your value, you won't compromise it for approval. when you know your worth, you won't trade it for half love. when you know your path, you won't wander into detours that drain you. the world will always try to hand you identities, labels, and expectations, but when you've spent time with yourself, when you've listened to your own voice long enough, you'll know which things to take in and which things to let pass through you. so take the time. learn yourself deeply. honor the parts of you that others overlook, because every moment you spend *understanding yourself is another layer of protection for the life you're building.* the stronger your sense of self, the softer it becomes to move through a world that is always trying to pull you away from it.

DECEMBER 28TH

if it isn't going to plan,
that's a divine sign, too.
pay attention.

when you've done all you can and put in the necessary effort that you think a situation requires, find no shame in surrendering and following the path of least resistance when nothing is flowing in the direction you need it to. the lack of alignment you feel is your guiding source, *it's a divine sign that whatever you seek can't be forced into being found,* it's a subtle reminder that what is for you will always find you, and what isn't should be released to make space for what is eventually meant to come.

DECEMBER 29TH

when the waves show you where you stand with certain people, don't resist the current. let the clarity wash over you.

open your eyes when people's true intentions are revealed, resist ignoring the signs when your intuition reveals the truth, accept what people show you even when their words suggest something different. sometimes it's not the hope of having stronger connections in relationships that we need to wish for; rather, we should hope to gain the awareness to recognize red flags and the courage to never look back when the unfiltered picture is revealed.

DECEMBER 30TH

detach as many times as you need,
let go as many times as you need,
release as many times as you need
until you start to feel like you again.

i hope you never fall into the habit of holding on to what has passed its sell-by date and what no longer wants to hold on to you; i hope you resist becoming too attached to what can't be changed and what is asking to be released. everything that's gone is no longer around for good reason, and everyone that's out of your reach is away from your grasp for good reason. accept things for what they are without letting regret keep you stuck in the past, accept things for what they are without letting guilt halt your progress, accept things for what they are without trying to resurrect what's expired. *hold gratitude for the lessons old connections taught you so you can create space for everything better that you deserve to attract.*

DECEMBER 31ST

let a beautiful new life happen to you.

sometimes we lose track of our self-worth when we indulge in certain connections, sometimes we lose sight of our sense of self when we pursue certain opportunities, sometimes we move further away from ourselves when we chase illusions and shadows that don't belong to us, and sometimes we dilute our essence when we take on responsibilities that aren't ours. so many things threaten to pull us further away from who we are or who we're trying to be, but nothing feels better than coming back to where you belong after being in the dark or the wilderness for so long, nothing feels better than remembering your worth again after it was lost for a brief period of time. *there's nothing more powerful than finally realizing that everything you could ever need already exists within you.*

stay in your magic, now and forever.

ABOUT THE AUTHOR

billy chapata is a zimbabwean writer, artist, and creative based in atlanta, georgia. he immigrated to the united states during his late adolescent years, but writing has been a staple for him throughout his entire life. having lived in various countries ranging from china to kenya, chapata's exposure to different cultures allows for deeply informed thoughts and writing that reflect on a wide spectrum of experiences. touching on topics of healing, self-love, and growth, his work aims to help people find a way back to themselves through poetry-infused words and sentiments.

The authorised representative in the EEA is Simon and Schuster Netherlands BV, Herculesplein 96 3584 AA Utrecht, Netherlands. (info@simonandschuster.nl)

Andrews McMeel Publishing
a division of Andrews McMeel Universal
1130 Walnut Street, Kansas City, Missouri 64106

www.andrewsmcmeel.com

26 27 28 29 30 SDB 10 9 8 7 6 5 4 3 2 1

ISBN: 979-8-8816-0533-9

Library of Congress Control Number: 2026934451

Editor: Danys Mares
Art Director: Julie Barnes
Production Editor: Kayla Overbey
Production Manager: Julie Skalla

FSC
www.fsc.org
MIX
Paper | Supporting responsible forestry
FSC® C144853